T0367953

A JOURNEY TOWARDS
ENDLESS LIGHT
OUT OF PITILESS
DARKNESS

A JOURNEY TOWARDS
ENDLESS LIGHT
OUT OF PITILESS DARKNESS

A COLLECTION OF SONNETS, LIMERICKS, OTHER POEMS AND SHORT STORIES

RAY OROCCO-JOHN

ARCHWAY
PUBLISHING

Archway Publishing books may be ordered through booksellers or by contacting:

Archway Publishing
1663 Liberty Drive
Bloomington, IN 47403
www.archwaypublishing.com
844-669-3957

ISBN: 978-1-6657-6058-4 (sc)
ISBN: 978-1-6657-6059-1 (e)

Library of Congress Control Number: 2024910486

Print information available on the last page.

Archway Publishing rev. date: 06/06/2024

CONTENTS

Presented To

FOREWORD

This anthology fuses an array of poems and short stories, meticulously crafted over many years. It spans a diverse spectrum of themes—from the lighthearted whimsy of comedy to the profound depths of everyday human experiences. The author presents a distinctive perspective on biblical scriptures, enriching them with personal insights and reflections. Moreover, this collection acts as a reflective mirror, capturing the essence of pivotal events and characters that have left an indelible mark on the author's life journey.

In homage to the Bard, the author has skillfully crafted a series of sonnets that honor both the traditional Shakespearean style and the lyrical Italian form. Adding a touch of whimsy, the book includes a selection of limericks, initially penned in jest but now presented for the readers' delight.

The short stories explore themes of unrequited love, sacrifice, forgiveness, fractured vows, the resilience of the human spirit, the devastating impact of war on innocent children, heartbreak, resurgence, the fallibility of human judgment, enduring love, jealousy, and the pain of abandonment. Each story conveys a message that resonates deeply with the reader.

The book's title reflects the author's transformative journey from the shadows of adversity to the radiant light of divine grace. This profound metamorphosis is delicately woven into the fabric of the poetry and prose, offering readers an intimate glimpse into the soul of a writer reborn. This work is the second installment in a series, following the author's initial offering, "Of Sadness and Of Pleasure."

DEDICATION

This book is dedicated to my family and friends, whose unwavering support has been my anchor. Also, to those I have wronged in the past and those who wronged me, for each interaction has been a lesson and a step towards growth. To the strangers who have inspired me and the mentors who have shaped me, I appreciate you for being essential fibers that constitute the quilt of my being.

And to the future generations who may wander through these pages, may you find solace, inspiration, and the courage to dream.

SHORT STORIES

1

An Enduring Love

Matthew Chung, known as Matt to friends and family, crossed paths with Lilly Yang at a prestigious school for gifted and affluent students. Their backgrounds couldn't have been more different: Matt, a prince from a lineage that had ruled a small region nestled among remote, towering mountains in Asia for generations; and Lilly, the daughter of poor rice farmers who lived thirty miles away from her school. The poor family had used their savings to send their gifted daughter, Lilly, to this prestigious school. Despite their disparate origins, Matt and Lilly's connection was destined.

From the moment Matt laid eyes on Lilly, he was captivated. Her natural beauty transcended her humble family background. Her bluish-green eyes held both keen intelligence and serene wisdom, casting an enchanting spell on anyone who met her. Lilly's grace defied her modest beginnings, and her demeanor mirrored that of a noblewoman.

Throughout their school days, Matt and Lilly were inseparable. They studied together, shared meals, and embarked on long walks along the mountain trails surrounding their campus. The lush greenery enveloped them, providing solace and inspiration. When they weren't buried in textbooks, they reveled in the beauty of their surroundings.

One rainy day, as they strolled the trails, Lilly abandoned her umbrella and turned her face to the falling rain with carefree delight, an insouciant joy. Matt followed suit, discarding his own umbrella. They stood together, drenched, their clothes clinging like a second skin. It was a moment of pure joy, the kind that comes from knowing you're loved and that your feelings are reciprocated.

Their courtship was the envy of their friends. Matt was certain that Lilly was his soulmate, and he vowed to marry her after college, regardless of life's challenges. Lilly, too, was equally enchanted by Matt. Their love story unfolded against the backdrop of mist-shrouded mountains, rain-kissed leaves, and the promise of a shared future, come rain or shine.

On some occasions, they would write poems to each other expressing their love and admiration. Lilly once wrote to Matt:

My heart forever joined with yours,
    Like water to the sea,
Our joys forever one, because
    Without you, I'm not me.

I've kissed the sun and moon and stars
    Quite often in my dreams,
Yet, none of these your kiss compares;
    Your lips are joyous streams.

And Matt responded to Lilly, writing:

You are my waterfall of peace,
    And river flowing joy;
Where meets the two, love's show'rs release
    For my soul to enjoy.

You are the wonder of my days,
    Dreamlike, yet fully true,
This heart of mine is yours and says,
    "Forever, I'll love you."

After college, Matt stood before his parents, his heart aflutter with vulnerable hope. He unveiled the depths of his soul, confessing his love for Lilly, his chosen soulmate. With each word, he laid bare his dreams of a shared future, his voice a tremulous wave cutting through the silence.

But the response that echoed back was a tempest of disapproval, especially from his father, the king, whose words thundered like a gavel against Matt's aspirations. "Not so fast," the king bellowed, his decree slicing through the air like a cold blade. "Marriage to a commoner is an affront to our lineage, a disruption of centuries-old traditions and laws. We must seek a bride of royal blood to uphold the sanctity of our throne."

The gravity of his father's words was a crushing blow, a maelstrom that swallowed Matt's flickering light of joy. He had yearned for a celebration, for the warm embrace of acceptance. Instead, he found himself in the eye of a storm, pelted by the relentless downpour of rejection. His father's heart, encased in the iron grip of tradition, refused to yield to the tender pleas of his son's heart.

In the days that followed, Matt was a ghost among the living, his spirit frayed and worn. The taste of food turned to ash on his tongue, sleep became a stranger, and even the sweetest drink could not quench his parched soul. His family's ultimatum loomed over him like a dark cloud—conform or be cast out into the abyss of solitude.

The relentless siege upon his will threatened to erode his resolve. Matt's mind was a battlefield, his love for Lilly the flag still flying amidst the smoke and ruin. Would he stand firm, a defiant beacon against the storm, or would the relentless waves of tradition and duty wash away the very essence of his being?

On that fateful day, as the sun's last rays kissed the horizon, Lilly and Matt found themselves on a hill cradling their village in its gentle slope. The dying light cast long shadows across the land, mirroring the somber shade falling upon their hearts. They held each other in a desperate embrace, tears carving rivers of sorrow on their cheeks. Each sob was a wordless testament to the love they feared was doomed by an unseen, unfeeling fate. With heavy hearts, they parted, their souls etched with the memory of that twilight goodbye.

As seasons turned, Lilly's world was a canvas of muted colors, her days a series of motions without meaning. Yet, life, with its relentless pace, ushered her forward. Two years drifted by like leaves on a wayward breeze, and Lilly found herself in the gaze of another. A man whose interest was gently nurtured by Kathy, Lilly's lifelong confidante.

They settled into a home twenty miles from the clamor of the past. Lilly's path diverged from the one she had once walked with Matt, yet his memory was a ghostly presence, a whisper in the quiet moments, a silhouette in the corner of her eye. The ache for what could have been was a bittersweet companion, a silent acknowledgment that some loves, though lost, shape us forever.

As for Matt, he sought refuge in the bottle, drowning his pain in alcohol. He refused to marry the woman his family had chosen for him, defying their wishes. In return, they severed all ties, disowning him. His heartache became a silent anthem, echoing through the mountains and the halls of buildings that once witnessed their love, now thwarted by tradition, sacrifice, and the weight of a crown.

Each morning, Matt followed a well-worn path along the bank of a nearby river. This was the same route he had often walked with Lilly, and every step brought back memories, the bittersweet echoes of the love that slipped through his fingers. But the river remained, a silent witness to their shared moments.

The water flowed with a clarity that mirrored the purity of their connection. It originated from melted snow on a nearby mountain, cascading down in a gentle rush. Matt would stand there, staring into its depths, seeking solace. The river held many secrets including his and Lilly's, carried away by the current.

His face often wore the mask of sorrow, engraved with lines of longing. Thoughts of Lilly would flit through his mind, like fragile butterflies. For a fleeting moment, her memory would warm his heart, only to be replaced by tears, their salty trails mingling with the river's flow.

Lonely and starved of Lilly's warmth, Matt found refuge by the water's edge. The river became his confidante, absorbing his pain. It listened as he poured out his heart, the words tumbling forth like glum leaves and debris carried downstream. He spoke of love, of betrayal, of a future denied. The river, ancient and unyielding, bore witness to it all.

One day, in a haze of depression and alcohol, Matt stumbled to the riverbank. His voice slurred, he addressed the water as if it held the answers. "Why?" he asked. "Why must love be a curse? Why am I a pawn in this cruel game?" The river, ever patient, whispered back, "What will you do about it?"

His anger surged. "I curse you," he snarled. "May your flow cease, your banks wither. Let the rain and snow forget you." The river remained unmoved, its surface unbroken. It whispered again, "What will you do about it?" Matt's words hung in the air, a futile defiance against forces greater than himself.

And so, he left; the broken prince, the rejected lover, walking away from the river that had both consoled and challenged him. The water continued its journey, unswayed by human woes. Perhaps it carried his pain downstream, mingling it with the stories of countless others. Or perhaps it simply flowed, indifferent to the heartache etched into its banks.

The following week, Matt returned to the river, the water's surface now a mirror reflecting his inner turmoil. Sobriety had replaced the haze of alcohol, and he gazed at the unfamiliar face staring back at him. This was not the Matt who had captured Lilly's heart, nor the confident prince who once believed love could conquer all.

He praised the river, its currents weaving through his memories: "How beautiful are the streams that flow into you," he murmured, "how lovely the golden sun caressing your waters." The sun's rays danced on the surface, evoking images of playful moments with Lilly, the way her hair had felt under his fingertips, the laughter they shared. He then praised the river saying, "may you remain beautiful, the mountains and streams ever replenish you with fresh water from pure white snow."

Leaving the riverbank, responding to the river's earlier challenge, Matt made a drastic decision: he quit drinking cold turkey. His love for Lilly burned undiminished, fueling a newfound purpose. He embarked on a campaign to rewrite the village's laws, to challenge tradition and allow commoners and royals to marry. Door by door, he shared his story of the love lost, and his family's rejection. His passion resonated with those who listened.

And then, against all odds, his campaign succeeded. The king, affronted by Matt's defiance, had barred him from ascending the throne. But the villagers held power too. Their laws allowed periodic petitions and votes. They rallied behind Matt, their voices echoing through the streets and mountain coves. Overwhelmingly, they chose compassion over convention, love over lineage.

Matt's royal privileges were restored, not because of his bloodline, but because of his unwavering heart. The river flowed on, carrying whispers of change, of a love that had weathered storms and emerged stronger. And in the reflection, Matt glimpsed a new version of himself; one shaped by love, resilience, and the belief that even a prince could rewrite destiny.

Lilly, her heart a tempest of emotions, sat across from her old friend Kathy in the cozy confines of the local café. The air was thick with memories of their shared laughter, late-night study sessions, and the camaraderie that had once bound them while in boarding school. But today, Kathy bore a burden, a secret she could no longer carry.

As they sipped their sweet and sour soup and twirled noodles around their chopsticks, Kathy hesitated. The truth weighed heavily on her tongue, threatening to spill forth. Finally, she leaned in, her voice a fragile thread. "Lilly," she began, "there's something I've kept hidden for years."

Lilly's eyes narrowed. "What is it?" she asked, her curiosity piqued.

Kathy took a deep breath. "I was part of a plot, a web of deception spun by the king himself." Her words hung in the air, like the steam rising from their bowls. "Your husband," she continued, "was paid by Matt's father, the very king who rejected your love, to court you. It was all orchestrated to keep Matt away from you."

Lilly's chest tightened with emotion. The pieces fell into place; the inexplicable distance between her and Matt, the whispers that reached her ears. She had been a pawn in a game of power and tradition. Anger surged within her, a tempest threatening to engulf reason.

"Why?" she demanded, her voice trembling. "Why would they do this, Kathy?"

Kathy's gaze dropped. "The king believed that if you were in another man's arms, Matt would move on. That he'd forget you. Also, the king offered your husband cash towards your new home."

Lilly's fists clenched. "And what about my feelings? My heart?" she snarled. "Was that of no consequence?"

Kathy's eyes filled with regret. "I'm so sorry, Lilly. I never wanted to hurt you."

But Lilly had heard enough. She stood abruptly, her chair scraping against the floor. "I will never forgive you for this," she declared, her voice carrying across the café. She tossed cash onto the table for her portion of the bill and strode out, leaving behind the warmth of friendship and the bitter taste of betrayal.

Outside, rain began to fall, a cleansing deluge that matched the storm within her. She would confront her husband, face the truth head-on. And perhaps, just perhaps, she would find a way to rewrite her own destiny, one that didn't bow to kings or schemes, but to the fierce beating of her heart.

Lilly stormed into the dimly lit bar, her heart ablaze with fury. The door swung open as if propelled by a tempest, nearly toppling a lady who had been exiting. The patrons turned their heads, their conversations silenced by the sudden intrusion. But Lilly had no time for pleasantries.

Her eyes locked onto her husband, sitting huddled with his friends at a corner table. She lunged toward him, fingers clawing at his shirt, her voice a raw scream. "You took a bribe from the king!" she accused. "A bribe to marry me."

His friends exchanged bewildered glances, caught off guard by the drama unfolding before them. Her husband remained silent, his eyes darting between Lilly and the exit.

"He wooed me under false pretenses," she continued, her voice rising. "This devil," she yelled, gesturing toward him. "I can't believe I fell for your deceit."

With that, she spun on her heel and stormed out, the door slamming shut behind her, perhaps a punctuation mark on their shattered love. Rain pelted the pavement as she hurried home, her mind a tempest of emotions.

Back in their house, Lilly began packing. She folded memories into cardboard boxes; the laughter, the stolen kisses, the promises whispered in moonlit corners. The room echoed with her anger, a concerto of shattered dreams. This was not the genteel Lilly they knew, the one who had once danced through life with grace.

When her husband returned, the battle resumed. He pleaded, his words desperate. "It's not what it seems," he insisted. "I loved you from the moment I met you."

But Lilly was done. She hurled accusations, flung objects across the room. The walls absorbed her rage, bearing witness to a love unraveling. He explained, "it was the king's threats, the weight of tradition," but it was too late. Her heart had calcified.

Their parting was brutal. "Our relationship is over," she declared, her voice a blade. "I never want to see you again."

And so, she sought refuge in her aunt's house, a sanctuary where the rain tapped against the window, matching the rhythm of her tears. The following weeks blurred into a haze of grief and healing. Lilly, once a pawn in a royal game, now stood at the crossroads of her own destiny.

Lilly sat on a weathered bamboo bench, the sun's warmth kissing her skin in the tranquil backyard of her aunt's home. The air smelled of earth and memories—the kind that lingered long after the rain had passed. Her little niece, a whirlwind of energy, darted toward her, breathless and excited.

"Someone's here to see you!" the child exclaimed, her eyes wide with anticipation.

Lilly's heart skipped a beat. "If it's your uncle," she replied, her voice tinged with bitterness, "I have no desire to see him."

"No, no!" the niece corrected. "It's someone else."

Lilly's back remained turned to the entrance, but she sensed his presence—a familiar warmth, a gravitational pull. Matt. The man who had once been her everything. As if feeding oxygen to dying embers, she felt a spark ignite within her.

He approached silently, wrapping his arms around her. His touch spoke volumes—the ache of separation, the longing for what had been lost. Lilly's breath caught as he pressed a gentle kiss to her forehead. In that moment, words were unnecessary. She stared at him, her eyes saying what her lips couldn't: "I'm sorry for all I put you through."

But Matt, too, had his confessions. "I apologize," he murmured, his voice raw. "For the pain you endured from the rejection by my family."

Lilly's anger flared anew. "Your father's treachery," she snarled. "The king's manipulation."

He nodded, his face etched with the anger of discovery. "I know. But I'm undeterred." Matt pulled up another bamboo chair, sitting close. They talked for hours—their voices weaving through memories, regrets, and unspoken promises.

Lilly revealed how she'd learned of the king's bribe, her husband's betrayal. Matt listened, devastated yet resolute. His hand found hers, fingers intertwining. "We will be together," he vowed. "Nothing in this world will prevent it."

And so, they clung to each other; a love tested by tradition, fueled by defiance. When he finally left, Matt's hug lingered depicting a promise etched into the framework of their shared history. The sun dipped below the horizon, casting long shadows. But in that fading light, Lilly glimpsed a future; a love rewritten, a kingdom reshaped.

Lilly's anger seethed, fueled by her husband's deceit. His attempts at reconciliation fell on deaf ears as she had no room for forgiveness. How could she have been so gullible, falling for a man who betrayed her love? She dubbed him Judas, but in her heart, he was worse than the betrayer of Jesus. She wished for his demise, not merely once, but repeatedly, as if her hatred could multiply the executioner's axe.

The divorce papers were filed by Lilly, citing deceit and irreconcilable differences as the reasons. Six months later, she emerged from the legal battle, her heart scarred but resolute.

Three years had etched their marks upon the kingdom, leaving behind a trail of shifting alliances and whispered secrets. The once indomitable king now lay frail and fading, his once-mighty voice reduced to a mere tremor. The chamber, adorned with tapestries depicting battles won and lost, bore witness to the weight of time and regret.

Summoned by the king, Matt entered the room. The prince, who had defied tradition for love, knelt by the bedside. The air hung heavy with the scent of aged red Cedar wood and memories. Matt's heart gritted, his face stern as he faced the man who had shaped his destiny, both for better and worse.

He then turned his back on the king, a silent rebellion against the treachery that had torn their family apart. His eyes welled with unshed tears as he spoke, each word a blade honed by years of longing and betrayal. Staring at portraits of erstwhile kings and queens of this kingdom, "You took many years of happiness from me," Matt began, his voice steady but laced with pain. "You turned the entire family against me."

The king's once-proud features sagged, lines etched deep by guilt. "I would expect such cold-heartedness and deceit from an ordinary villain," Matt continued, his gaze unwavering. "But not from a noble. Grandma used to tell us that kings are like mini-gods, entrusted with great responsibilities for those in their care. The God I know is not a deceitful one."

The king's voice trembled as he apologized, the words scraping against his parched throat. "For the pain, the manipulation, the shattered dreams," he rasped.

Matt remained unyielding, now facing the king, "Apologize to Lilly," he demanded, his resolve unshaken. "She deserves closure."

His father's weakened form straightened, pride flickering in his eyes. "You are an impossible son," the king muttered, a mix of exasperation and grudging admiration.

"Perhaps so," Matt replied, his voice firm. "But right is right, and as leaders, we must set a bright example in doing what's right."

And so, the king acquiesced. Lilly was summoned, her footsteps echoing down the corridor. But fate, ever unpredictable, played its hand. The king's breath slipped away before she arrived, leaving behind a room heavy with missed chances and irreversible choices. Matt stood there, torn between duty and love, as the kingdom shifted once more, forever altered by the choices made in that dimly lit chamber. As he looked upon his father's still form, he realized the mantle of leadership was now his to bear. In this moment of profound loss, he understood that his reign would be defined not by the shadows of the past, but by the light he chose to cast upon his people.

Matt, now the rightful heir, stood before the people. Beside him, Lilly, his queen, radiated strength. Their love had rewritten the rules, reshaped the monarchy. The celebrations were flamboyant with the "people's king" ascending the throne. Crowds cheered, banners fluttered, and the air hummed with anticipation.

For Matt and Lilly, it was more than a coronation. It was an affirmation, a testament to enduring love. As they stood together, their hands intertwined, the smiling sun retreated below the horizon. The past had been rewritten, and the future beckoned in a kingdom transformed by love's audacity.

2

Echoes of Judgment

In the quiet suburbs of Burlington, Vermont, around 2010, a church stood as a testament to the town's history and enduring presence. Established in the early 1900s, it had been a beacon for the affluent— the textile magnate, the liquor store owner, the jewelry merchant, the investment banker, and generations of families who had made their mark in this town. Yet, as the years rolled by, the town's vibrancy had dimmed, marred by the creeping shadows of drug addiction and a rising tide of crime.

The church, once the heart of the community, now echoed with the silence of empty pews. Its new pastor, the reverend Nathan Armstrong, a man of faith and vision, called upon his flock, seeking to rekindle the spirit of fellowship through the modern-day pulpit of social media. He opened the church's doors to all in the community including the downtrodden. "After all," he proclaimed, "this is the essence of our Christianity."

But his words stirred a tempest of dissent among the congregation. Some members, viewing the church as a sanctuary of tradition, resisted changes that might disrupt their familiar fellowship. They feared that newcomers could transform the cherished customs that form the backbone of this esteemed assembly. "We cannot have those vagabonds in our midst. Moreover, it will drain the congregation's resources," declared Tom Smith, a wealthy investment banker, his voice laced with contempt. "Half of them are drunks," lamented Jim Johnson, the proprietor of a liquor store, "squandering their last dime on spirits. Is this the company we seek?" Others expressed worries about the impact of "unrestrained men and women" on their children.

Humans, in their peculiar ways, yearn for perfection in others, blind to the flaws within themselves. They sit in judgment, casting stones for a single misstep. The pastor was not blind to the irony: a wealthy banker, thriving on the fruits of commerce, resistant to sharing with the needy; a liquor merchant, profiting from the vice he deplores. Struck by the frigidity of his congregation, Pastor Armstrong sought solace in the sacred texts, echoing the apostle John's wisdom: "For he who possesses the world's riches, yet beholds his kin in want and hardens his heart, how can the essence of the Divine dwell within? Dear ones, let us not love in mere words or speech, but through actions and in truth."

His plea resonated in the silence, overlooked by the church's stalwarts. Yet, hope flickered as a few young, untainted hearts, untouched by cynicism, persuaded their elders to embrace the pastor's vision. And so, the doors opened, ever so slightly, to the possibility of renewal and grace.

Pastor Armstrong's journey began with a simple act of compassion, as he stepped through the doors of the homeless shelter. There, he was greeted by faces etched with the hardships of life, eyes reflecting stories untold. With each handout of clothing and food, he offered not just material aid but also a message of spiritual nourishment. His gentle invitations to the Sunday service were like outstretched hands, promising a haven within the church's nurturing embrace, where weary hearts could find a moment's peace and a flicker of redemption.

His mission continued the next day at Jim Johnson's liquor store, a place often frequented by those seeking to escape their troubles at the bottom of a bottle. The pastor navigated the store with tranquil resolve, his smile cutting through the gloom, a lighthouse of hope to those adrift in their sorrows. He spoke to each patron, not with judgment but with an open heart, offering them a place in the church community.

These visits were not mere gestures; they were the embodiment of the pastor's belief in action and faith made manifest. He saw beyond the present, envisioning a future where every lost and weary traveler could find a home in the church, a sanctuary where broken spirits could be mended through fellowship and divine love.

As the weeks unfolded, each bible study became a resonant echo of the pastor's call for open hearts, reinforcing his assurance that divine grace would shepherd their collective transformation. On a Sunday that would be etched in memory, the church's doors opened wide, embracing the souls from the shelter. Among them was Sam, whose unsteady gait and demeanor hinted at recent inebriation, yet whose spirit was alight with the embers of a childhood faith. He spoke of a melody from his youth, known only as the "And He" song. The organist, with a touch of inspiration, began to play "In the Garden," and as the familiar chorus — "And He walks with me, and He talks with me"—filled the air, a powerful, tearful unity blossomed within the congregation. Sam's tenor voice soared, resonating through the sanctuary's vaulted dome, a testament to the enduring power of faith and fellowship. As Sam's voice carried the hymn, it seemed to lift the spirits of all who heard, binding them in a moment of shared humanity and divine connection.

As the last notes of the hymn faded into a profound silence, the congregation felt a shared, palpable stillness. From this quietude, a lone figure stood, his silhouette etched against the stained glass. "My name is Timothy Johnson," he began, his voice not just heard, but felt—a visceral, trembling echo of vulnerability. "I am ensnared by the chains of drink, and have been for more years than I care to count. I came here in search of the family ties my late father left frayed and forgotten. I seek not just help, but salvation. I yearn for liberation from this relentless demon. Pray for me, not as a stranger, but as a brother." Moved by his plea, the congregation rose as one, their prayers forming an amalgam of hope and support, a collective cradle of faith and love.

Pastor Armstrong's message, a blend of scripture and sincerity, had become integrated into the church community. It was a message that transcended the walls of the sanctuary, reaching out to the most vulnerable, offering them not just solace but a sense of belonging. The service concluded not with a closing prayer, but with an open invitation to continue this journey together, to build a community where every member, regardless of their past, could find a place to call home. The visitors departed, leaving behind a silence filled with the promise of redemption and the power of community.

The day after Timothy Johnson's poignant plea at the church, he found himself back at the liquor store. This time, it was Jim Johnson, the proprietor, who initiated the conversation. "You mentioned you're from out of town," Jim inquired with newfound interest. "Where is home for you?"

"Essex," Timothy replied, a tinge of sorrow in his voice. "My father went to war and never returned. It's been just my mother and me, until she passed last year. That's when I left for here."

Later that evening, in the quiet solitude of his home, Jim Johnson felt a pull of curiosity and rummaged through his memories. He had received a letter from his brother containing a soldier's plea: "Please take care of Sarah, my dear wife, and my son, Timothy." At the time, Jim had turned away from this responsibility, tucking the letter away in his lockbox, never reaching out to his brother's family.

Now, holding the aged, faded paper, Jim's hands trembled as the weight of years of disregard pressed heavily upon his conscience. The revelation hit him like a thunderclap shaking the foundations of his world: the man he had dismissed as just another drunk was, in fact, his own nephew, a blood relation his brother had entrusted him to protect.

Upon reading the letter, Jim Johnson's heart surged with a tumultuous mix of regret and resolve. He dashed through the streets of the town, driven by a newfound purpose. In the dim light of a local bar that night, he found Timothy. The man he had once viewed through a lens of disdain now stood before him, not just a shadow from his past, but a living bridge to his brother's legacy, his own blood calling out for recognition and familial love.

"May I have a word?" Jim implored, his voice trembling with anticipation. "Who did you say your father was?" The question hung in the air, heavy with significance.

"Robert Johnson," Timothy replied, unaware of the unfolding revelation.

"And your mother?" Jim pressed, his heart pounding.

"Sarah Lee Johnson," Timothy said, a note of reverence in his voice. "She rests with the Lord now."

In that sacred moment, the truth dawned on Jim. The man before him was not just any soul adrift; he was family, the son of his brother, a nephew he never knew he had. After sharing hugs and shedding some tears of regret, an overwhelmed, Jim reached out to his wife, sharing the astonishing news.

In the months that followed, Jim dedicated himself to Timothy's recovery, guiding him through the shadows of addiction towards the light of sobriety. He also took the time to truly see his customers, understanding them not as "drunks" but as individuals with stories and silent battles, each deserving of compassion and understanding.

On a radiant summer day, the sun blazed in a cloudless sky, casting a warm, golden glow over the congregation gathered outside. The air was alive with the scent of fresh grass and the sound of laughter as the church's youth realized their vision of an open-air service, followed by a summer cookout. It was a scene painted with the vibrant hues of community and fellowship.

Excitedly, Milly Jones, the church treasurer, remarked with a twinkle in her eye, "It is an unprecedented crowd!" Her words carried the weight of shared success and the sweet anticipation of stories yet to unfold among the gathered souls.

"It is indeed," the pastor responded, his voice rich with pride and a hint of wonder. His eyes swept over the faces of his flock, each one a cherished note in the symphony of their shared faith. His vision of a church of the community and for the community was gradually taking shape, not just in the bricks and mortar, but in the hearts beating in unison under the summer sky.

The outreach had been extensive, the youth tapping into the pulse of the digital age with social media, radio, and television. And as the service concluded, the anticipation for the cookout was palpable. It was then that Sam, the man whose soulful plea for "In the Garden" had once moved the congregation, stepped forward. His voice, now steady and clear, rose in a solo that soared above the gathered crowd, accompanied by the gentle strumming of a guitarist. The congregation's voices joined his in the chorus, their harmonies spilling into the summer air, a sacred symphony that seemed to touch the very gates of heaven.

This time, Sam stood before them, not as a man haunted by his past, but as a father, sober and resolute, with his son and daughter by his side. The cookout hummed with the energy of new connections, and it was here that Sam introduced his children to the pastor, standing next to Tom Smith, the investment banker. "These are your kids?" asked a surprised Tom Smith, his face lighting up with recognition. "Yes, sir," replied a proud father, Sam. Tom recounted how Sam's son, walking home from school one day, had stopped to help him install his spare tire when he had a flat on a nearby road.

Tom, confronted by the memory of his earlier judgment, felt a stirring of conscience. As the day's festivities wound down, he approached Sam with a humility that had eluded him before. "I was wrong," Tom confessed, "and my judgment was severely flawed. You have raised your children to be kind and thoughtful, and for that, you must be proud."

Sam, with a grace born of trials overcome, deflected the praise to their mother. "She has been their rock," he said, his voice tinged with gratitude and love, "and has stood by me as I battled my demons. I thank God for the strength to overcome."

With a handshake that sealed a newfound respect, the two men parted ways, leaving behind a day that would long be remembered—a testament to the power of forgiveness, the strength of community, and the enduring hope of transformation.

The church's doors opened wider, welcoming those who had once been outsiders. The congregation grew, not just in numbers, but in spirit and understanding. The town itself began to heal, its people united by a common purpose and a shared humanity.

It is often through the eyes of the young that we are reminded of our shared humanity—a humanity that is not without its imperfections, but is also ripe with the possibility of making amends and finding common ground. The youth, with their unclouded vision and inherent optimism, reveal to us the true fabric of life, one that is not stitched together with threads of contempt, but rather interlaced with ribbons of gratitude and the bright hues of hope.

Tom Smith, in his quiet moment and his newfound conviction, penned a poem about judging others, which reads:

The Garden Of Grace

In life's garden, where judgments grow,
We cast our seeds, yet we don't know,
    The roots take hold, but truth lies deep,
    In soils of hearts, where harsh views seep.

A rose may wilt before it blooms,
Under the weight of assumed glooms,
    Yet, who are we to judge the flow'r,
    When God, the gard'ner has that pow'r?

Each soul of man, a hidden tale,
A battle fought within the veil,
    And who are we to weigh their worth,
    When we share the same fragile Earth?

We'll grow with kindness, not disdain,
From hasty judgments, must refrain,
    For in the light of mercy's sun,
    We'll clearly see that we are one.

Six months had passed, and the church had become an indelible part of the community's social weave. Pastor Armstrong's vision of a sanctuary that truly opened its arms to all was nearly tangible, a dream delicately balanced on the cusp of reality. Yet, he could sense the undercurrents of reluctance pulsing through his congregation. The weary and worn, in search of a sliver of peace within the church's embrace, were often met with glares as cold and unyielding as marble statues, echoes of an era when centurions stood guard, unapproachable and stern. Among the faithful, there were those who mirrored the Pharisees of old, their hands clutching the sacred texts while their hearts remained closed, their interpretation of scripture laced with the thorns of judgment rather than the blossoming roses of grace and humility.

But within this haze of tradition and resistance, sparks of hope glistened—most brightly among the youth. These young souls saw beyond the church's ancient stones; they envisioned a beacon of hope, a lighthouse guiding towards a horizon where faith was not a fortress but a bridge, inviting new journeys and fresh perspectives within the Christian faith. It was this flicker of promise, this spark of understanding, that kept the flame of Pastor Armstrong's dream alight, even in the face of the gathering dusk of doubt.

At an elders' meeting, the church's financial head, James Carlisle, voiced his opposition to a proposal for monthly stipends to financially struggling newcomers. His words were laced with contempt: "We are now funding the addictions of drunks and drug users." The pastor sat, a mix of astonishment and disappointment washing over him. His message of compassion had resonated with some, but others remained untouched. That night, he left the meeting heavy-hearted, contemplating a strategy to win over the dissenters.

The following week, as the pastor prepared to address James' previous disparaging remarks, Tom Smith interjected, his voice cutting through the uncertainty. "Pastor, may I offer my voice on the matter of my friend, James' remarks?" he asked, his tone imbued with a sincerity that stilled the room. "I stand before you, a man who once cast a skeptical eye on those we labeled unworthy. Yet, through grace, I've come to understand that our calling is not to cast stones but to cast light—to illuminate our paths and those of our neighbors. If any among us can gaze upon the heavens and discern the stars destined to shine brightest tomorrow, let them be our guide. Otherwise, let us join hands in support, for every soul deserves a chance to rise." The pastor, visibly touched by Tom's heartfelt plea, felt a resurgence of faith wash over him. The elders, once divided, found unity in the warmth of Tom's wisdom, nodding in agreement to the stipends—a testament to the power of compassion over judgment.

That evening, the pastor shared with his wife a heartfelt revelation: his vision of a church free from prejudice was coming to life. He believed his congregation was ready to champion the virtues of inclusion, bridging divides with compassion and reaching out to those in need. "It is through aiding others in Christ's name that we find transformation and salvation," he confided. Together, they realized that in changing the lives of others, their own lives were also being uplifted and transformed.

Meanwhile, Kathy Coker, one of the people who had concerns about the influence of "unrestrained men and women" on our children, found herself unexpectedly, yet profoundly, in love with Timothy Johnson, a man who has triumphantly battled alcoholism. Kathy, once wounded by a former husband who mistreated her and vanished, leaving her to raise their daughter alone, now radiates with joy. Kathy and Timothy, now inseparable lovebirds, are planning to wed in a few months—on the very birthday of Kathy's cherished daughter. This date was chosen as a heartfelt tribute to the young girl's innocent prayer, which she whispered to the heavens: "I deserve a dad who loves me, Lord. For my tenth birthday, please bless my mum with a partner who will cherish us both." It seems the heavens have listened; her prayers have been tenderly answered. Since the blossoming of Timothy and Kathy's romance, he has embraced the role of a doting figure in the young girl's life, often seen patiently assisting her with homework and sharing in their laughter. Their bond is a testament to the healing power of love and the unexpected joys that life can bring.

3

Fractured Vows

Dan Churchill, a kind and loving husband, lived with his lovely wife of three years in the suburbs of Grand Rapids, Michigan. Their home was nestled in a beautiful neighborhood, surrounded by high-end single-family brick houses with spectacularly manicured lawns and soaring front porches. It was December 2019, and Dan was due for his annual eye exam. As a nearsighted individual, he had been wearing prescription eye contact lenses for about ten years. His trusted eye doctor, Dr. Louise Mantle, suggested a different brand of contacts than the ones Dan had been accustomed to. However, after a week of wearing the new lenses, an irritation in Dan's eyes prompted him to remove them temporarily. Unfortunately, by week's end, the damage was already done. The contact lenses had left a scar on Dan's right cornea and torn his left cornea. His eyesight was gradually slipping away.

Concerned, Dan reached out to Dr. Mantle, who referred him to an eye surgeon named Dr. Primosch. Despite Dr. Primosch's confidence that Dan could regain his eyesight, there was a lingering worry that the process might take some time. Meanwhile, Dan's wife, Kayla, a seasoned nurse with fifteen years of experience, stood by his side. She drove him to his appointments and expressed concern about the financial toll Dan's inactivity might take. Dan reassured her, emphasizing that with her support, things would eventually return to normal. Fortunately, the couple had a rainy day fund of about fifty thousand dollars, which could sustain them until Dan could get back on his feet.

Dan underwent three successful surgeries: the first to correct the damage to his eyes and the subsequent ones to replace his corneas. During his recovery, he grappled with both physical pain and emotional distress. His once mundane routines became arduous tasks, and Kayla found herself taking on additional responsibilities beyond what Dan typically handled. They had always functioned as a team, but Dan's unfortunate accident strained their relationship. Kayla's behavior shifted abruptly; she began leaving Dan at home to fend for himself. This change was surprising, especially given her background as a compassionate nurse.

As Dan coped with excruciating pain, he received narcotics to ease his discomfort. However, instead of relief, the drugs brought on frightening nightmares. One evening, after taking his medication, Dan sleepwalked through the house, hearing the unsettling chatter of a man and a woman engaged in what seemed like a sexual rendezvous. On another night, he dreamt of men in biker attire urging him to join them on a crime spree. Throughout this ordeal, Kayla remained distant—moving out of their shared bedroom and sleeping in the guest room. She was no longer available to meet Dan's needs, leaving him feeling abandoned and confused. He wondered if their once blossoming love could melt away under the heat of adversity. Questions plagued his mind: Was Kayla planning to leave him? Was she having an affair? How had he missed this side of her before they were married?

Most mornings, Dan would hear Kayla wake up and leave for work, shutting the front door behind her. In the evenings, she returned home, often engrossed in phone conversations with friends. Meanwhile, Dan fended for himself, navigating a world of uncertainty and longing for the warmth of their shared love.

Enter Maria Henton, the nurse sent by the staffing agency. Maria embodied everything one could ask for in a nurse: caring, attentive, and genuinely sweet. Beyond her nursing duties, she assisted Dan with writing letters, managing bills, and other mundane tasks. As the pain abated over the next three months, Dan adjusted to his blindness. He dictated a poignant poem, which Maria dutifully recorded:

A Blind Man's View

Reaching, feeling for simple needs,
    Sleep-walking the unknown,
Pondering sprouting blooms from seeds,
    I embrace as my own.

Imagining the beautiful,
    Old yardsticks prick my mind.
Dreaming all things are wonderful
    Is feature of my kind.

Blackness in every corner roves,
    Firm as the morning sun,
Hides mountains, seas, except my vibes;
    Eager to have some fun.

Although I try to disregard
   Dark shadows in my paths,
Often I'm shattered, tired, and sad,
   From lasting overcasts.

Wishing these wicked clouds would cease
   To dominate my sun;
From its dungeon, grant my release,
   And dreary days be gone.

After six months caring for Dan, Maria, with her heart full of compassion, pondered the mystery of Kayla's abandonment during Dan's most vulnerable moments. She thought about broaching the subject with Kayla, but grappled with the boundaries of her professional role, torn between duty and genuine concern.

One summer day, with the sun bright and the air sun baked, Dan asked Maria to take him out for a ride in her old Toyota Corolla sedan. On that particular sun-kissed afternoon, they drove to Lincoln Park, a haven of natural beauty just five miles from Dan's house. The park unfolded before them—luscious greenery, sunlight filtering through leaves, an abundance of birds and ducklings in ponds, and the distant hum of life at a creek. A weathered bench beckoned, and there, like a scene from a bittersweet play, sat Kayla with another man's arms wrapped around her neck.

Maria acted swiftly, guiding a blind Dan away from the painful scene. They settled on the grass on the opposite end of the park, sharing prepared sandwiches—their simple sustenance a comforting balm. This section of the park became their sanctuary, a place where they could explore without fear of crossing paths with Kayla. Amidst the rustling leaves and the distant laughter of children playing games, Maria and Dan forged a bond—a silent promise to protect each other from life's storms. Dan had a great time and thanked Maria for spending time with him at the park.

As the weeks unfolded, Dan and Maria delved into each other's lives. One evening, prompted by Dan's curiosity, Maria revealed that she was thirty-five years old and divorced. Her ex-husband had run off with a younger woman, leaving Maria to navigate the aftermath of shattered dreams. She spoke with a hint of sarcasm: "I guess he wanted to resume sowing his wild oats." They shared a laugh, finding solace in humor amidst life's trials.

Dan, intrigued by Maria's patience and kindness, confessed, "I can sense your beauty, Maria. God grants outward beauty to those with hearts like yours." Maria received his words like a delicate flower, her response a blend of grace and insight. "Appearances can be deceiving," she mused, "and beauty without substance is but an empty vessel."

Dan pondered her words, reflecting on his own experience. "My former husband," Maria admitted, "falls squarely into that category. He was handsome and the epitome of charm, yet beneath the veneer, he was nothing but falsehood and infidelity."

And so, amidst shared laughter and unspoken promises, Dan and Maria's bond deepened—a testament to the unseen beauty that blossomed between them.

One midnight, Dan was abruptly awakened from his slumber by the sound of his wife, Kayla, engaged in an argument with a man in a nearby bedroom. "Is that you, Kayla?" he shouted, concern etching his voice. Kayla's curt response cut through the darkness: "Go to sleep; you're having nightmares again." Dan chose not to escalate the situation and settled back into his restless slumber.

On a scorching August day, at Dan's request, Maria drove him to Lincoln Park. The sun beat down, but a gentle breeze tempered the humidity. They settled once again on the grass, surrounded by flitting birds. Tossing peanuts to their feathered companions, they savored prepared sandwiches—the simple pleasure of shared meals.

Suddenly, Dan's voice broke the tranquility: "Maria, that's a Blue Jay." His assertion was spot-on; the bird's vibrant plumage confirmed it. Maria, aware of Dan's lost eyesight, chose not to acknowledge his observation. But within seconds, Dan asserted again: "Maria, that's a Cardinal." This time, Maria agreed, "Yes, it is, Dan." Perhaps, against all odds, Dan was slowly regaining his sight.

After their meal, they strolled through the park, Maria describing the contours Dan couldn't fully perceive. The memories flooded back—this very park where he and Kayla had once walked hand in hand during their dating years. Dan wondered what had happened to that love, but he found solace in Maria's presence. Her kindness surpassed anything he'd experienced, even from his wife. As they drove home, Dan rolled down the car windows, soaking in the warmth of summer—the unseen beauty of a life reshaped by love and resilience.

That evening, after Kayla left for work, Dan rose to use the bathroom. His hand found the light switch, and suddenly, he glimpsed his own image in the mirror. His vision remained blurry, but he could see again. Suppressing the urge to scream in excitement, he waited for Kayla's return.

At 11:30 PM, the front door swung open. Dan stood at the top of the staircase, ready to share the good news with his wife. But what he witnessed shattered his fragile hope: Kayla, entangled with another man, their passion evident as they entered the house, locking lips, shedding clothes, and inhibitions. The air thickened with betrayal, suffocating Dan's heart.

Dan's soft call— "Kayla"—was met with a dismissive response: "Go to bed, you're sleepwalking again." The words cut through him like shards of glass. His newfound sight had revealed more than he bargained for.

In his bedroom, Dan waited with a heavy heart. Kayla and her paramour ascended the stairs, their footsteps leading to the guest bedroom. The bed creaked under their weight, a cruel symphony of deceit. Dan's mind raced, replaying memories of their life together—the laughter, the shared dreams, the whispered promises. How long had she been carrying this affair? The pieces fell into place: the times he was in pain, and Kayla would increase his dosage, insisting it would help. Was she trying to get him to sleep so she could explore her trysts?

The muffled noises from the guest bedroom reached Dan's ears—an argument, perhaps. He clenched his fists, torn between confronting them and preserving the illusion of bliss. The darkness that had once enveloped him now revealed Kayla's hidden heart—the shadows he'd never suspected. Her dark side, laid bare. A surge of anger swept over him, and for a moment, he considered reaching for his weapon—a silver handgun. Yet, he dismissed the thought as reckless. Violence had never been his way, and this revelation of Kayla's betrayal would not alter his character. His anger subsided as he contemplated his next move.

Dan grabbed his phone, activated the video function, and recorded the encounter—the damning evidence of betrayal. The screen blurred as tears welled up. He retreated to his dimly lit bedroom, lying on his bed, staring at portraits of their wedding. The smiles frozen in time mocked him. The love they once shared now twisted into a bitter knot.

As the night wore on, Dan grappled with his emotions. The video was his weapon, but it also weighed heavy on his soul. He wondered if he'd ever trust again, if love could survive such treachery. The dawn approached, casting a feeble light through the curtains. Dan closed his eyes, replaying the scene—the mirror, the footsteps, the whispered lies. It took his blindness to see the truth: Kayla was no longer the woman he thought he knew.

The next day, Maria arrived. Dan opened the door, finally seeing the woman who had turned his nightmare around. Her bluish-green eyes and flowing hair captivated him. He complimented her beauty, affirming that God bestowed it upon special souls. Tearfully, Maria hugged him, sharing in his joy.

Dan recounted the previous night's events to Maria, showing her the recording. She empathized with his pain. "What will you do?" she asked. Dan's resolve was clear: Kayla, selfish and self-centered, had discarded their once-budding love. He would seek a divorce.

That evening, he sat in his chair, waiting for Kayla's return. When she walked through the door, Dan delivered the news: "Honey, I've regained my eyesight." Kayla's response— "I'm happy for you"—rang hollow. Dan pressed further: "Are you really? Because you don't seem like it." Kayla's anger flared: "Stop the games. Our marriage ended long ago. You couldn't give me what I wanted." Dan's calm retort— "Thank you, dear"—sealed their fate. Kayla moved out, and the once-blossoming love lay shattered, like a fragile mirror reflecting broken images.

The following week, Dan contacted his employer, informing them of his recovery and imminent return to work. Then he called his attorney, instructing the filing of divorce papers based on Kayla's infidelity.

Dan continued his meetings with Maria, their connection deepening with each passing day. They went on several dates, exploring the intricacies of their hearts. That autumn, they found themselves at Lincoln Park to soak in nature's artistry. The wind choreographed a dance of fiery leaves under a cloudless sky. They sat on a blanket, sharing prepared tuna sandwiches, potato chips, and colas—their favorite combination. Dan poured out his love for Maria, vowing to marry her once his divorce was finalized. Maria reciprocated, confessing her feelings for the man she had cared for so tenderly. She described him as thoughtful, gentle, and sweet.

Maria also revealed the incident involving Kayla and her friend at the park. She had kept it from Dan, hoping to shield him from the pain such a revelation might bring. Grateful for her thoughtfulness, Dan sealed the evening with a kiss before they drove back home.

Together, Dan and Maria embarked on a marvelous journey across continents. They explored Europe, Africa, and Asia, marveling at the Great Wall of China, Victoria Falls at the border between Zambia and Zimbabwe, the Austrian Alps, and other captivating destinations in Bulgaria and Germany. Their steps were in sync, hearts beating as one. No longer did Maria guide Dan through traffic or up and down stairs. Instead, they walked hand in hand, a testament to their shared love.

Dan marveled, "Maria gave me more love in a week than Kayla did throughout our entire time together. Perhaps the Man in heaven is looking out for me."

A year after the finalization of Dan's divorce from Kayla, he stood before the altar once more. True to his promise, he married Maria on a crisp Christmas morning—the air infused with the promise of new beginnings. The Christmas day wedding was Maria's special wish. The church, adorned with evergreen wreaths and flickering candles, welcomed them into its hallowed embrace.

As the organ played a melodic hymn, Dan's eyes found Maria. Her gown, a cascade of ivory lace, whispered promises of forever. They exchanged vows with words etched in their hearts, binding them anew. The congregation watched, their breaths held, as Dan slipped a ring onto Maria's finger completing their circle of an unbroken commitment.

After the beautiful church service, the couple led their guests to a lavish reception at a grand banquet hall. The room shimmered with Christmas magic: ornaments hung from chandeliers, tinsels adorned every corner, and bows graced each chair. The scent of pine mingled with the aroma of festive delicacies.

Dan and Maria danced their first dance in a divinely romantic waltz that transcended time. The notes of "Silent Night" swirled around them, and for a moment, they were suspended in a snow globe of love. Friends and family joined them, twirling under the twinkling lights, celebrating the union of two souls who had weathered storms and emerged stronger.

As midnight approached, snow began to fall outside, cloaking the world in purity. Dan held Maria close, whispering promises against her hair. They stepped out into the frost-kissed night, hand in hand, leaving the banquet hall behind. The snowflakes danced around them, weaving their story into the magic of the season—a tale of fractured vows mended by love's gentle touch.

And so, on that Christmas Day, Dan and Maria embarked on a new chapter, finding solace in each other's arms.

Later, Dan discovered the painful truth: Kayla's love interest was none other than Naomi's husband, John. Jealousy had fueled Kayla's actions, and she sought to hurt her friend by engaging in an affair with her husband. Kayla hoped that John would leave Naomi for her, but reality didn't align with her desires. Naomi eventually caught them in a compromising situation at her home and revealed Kayla's betrayal to their circle of friends.

In the aftermath, Naomi and her husband embarked on a journey of healing through therapy, ultimately reconciling. Meanwhile, Kayla faced the consequences of her actions; she was alone, having lost both Dan and Naomi's husband. The tangled web of love, betrayal, and friendship had left scars that time alone could begin to heal.

4

Forgiveness is a Mighty Stream

The chilling winds of that November evening swept through the Goldberg household, leaving behind an emptiness that no warmth could fill. Janice Goldberg, a mother who had cradled dreams for her daughter, now clung to memories like fragile threads. Jane, her nineteen-year-old daughter, had vanished into the night, leaving a void that echoed with unanswered questions.

The clock struck 9 pm, and the walls of their home seemed to close in on Janice. Jane's absence was an anomaly, a deviation from the familiar rhythm of their life. The door remained unopened, the hallway devoid of her laughter and chats about her workday. Jane, who had always returned home promptly at 5 pm, was now lost in the shadows.

Desperation drove Janice to dial Jane's friends, one by one. Their voices trembled over the phone lines, recounting those mundane moments such as the glimpses of Jane at work, the casual exchanges, the shared laughter. Each friend unwittingly became a witness to the unraveling mystery. Jane had left her workplace, they confirmed, heading home as usual. But where was she now?

The local grocery store which stood a few miles away was a beacon of familiarity in their small community. Jane had mentioned stopping there for organic vegetables. Janice's heart raced as she relayed this detail to the police. Their investigation began, fueled by urgency and dread. Every second stretched into eternity, and Janice clung to hope, praying for Jane's safe return.

In the stillness of the night, when shadows merged with silence and the world surrendered to dreams, the shrill ring of the phone shattered the calm. It was 2 am, a time when darkness reigns and fears loom larger. The call was an omen, a grim herald that something was amiss. Janice's heart raced as she answered, her hand trembling with a foreboding chill.

The officer on the other end spoke with a gravity that weighed heavily in the air, his words deliberate and somber. Each syllable was a hammer, chiseling the devastating news into Janice's soul, leaving indelible marks of sorrow. Jane, her cherished daughter, the beacon of her life, had been subjected to a heinous act, her vibrant spirit snuffed out.

The woods, once a sanctuary of tranquility where birdsong filled the air and leaves danced in the wind, had become a silent witness to the atrocity. They now cradled Jane's lifeless form—a daughter, a friend, a dreamer—abandoned in the cold embrace of the earth. Discarded as if her laughter, her hopes, her very essence meant nothing. Betrayed by the world she had trusted, her stillness screamed louder than any cry for help.

Janice's world, once colored with the hues of Jane's love, now collapsed into a monochrome of pain. The loss was a void no words could fill, a wound no time could heal. As the officer continued, each fact was a dagger, each detail a theft of the future they would never share. Janice clutched the phone, her knuckles white, as tears streamed down her face, each one a testament to the love she bore for her daughter—a love that would endure beyond death's cruel parting.

The night air, thick with the scent of pine and sorrow, whispered Jane's name. And in that moment, Janice knew that while the world might continue to spin, her own had irrevocably stopped, anchored in the memory of the daughter she adored.

The Goldbergs' home became a sanctuary of grief. The kind of grief that blocks the sun even at noon on the brightest day. Janice and her husband huddled together, their tears mingling with disbelief. Jane, their only child, had been stolen from them, a bright star extinguished by darkness. She had dreams and lofty aspirations of becoming a nurse practitioner, and was working at a bookstore to save money for expenses during Nursing school which awaited her in January, a path now forever untrodden.

Jane's friends remembered her as convivial and conversational, her opinions firm yet compassionate. Her presence ignited discussions, turning casual gatherings into spirited debates. But now, those gatherings felt incomplete, the laughter hollow. The room echoed with the absence of her voice, the void of her smile.

In the wake of tragedy, the Goldbergs grappled with loss; the pain of a parent's shattered hopes, the ache of a stolen future. Jane's memory lingered in every corner, a fragile flame flickering against the darkness. And as the cold winds whispered through their home, Janice clung to the fragments of her daughter's existence, yearning for justice, solace, and the impossible return of what was lost.

In the days that followed, the community rallied around the Goldbergs, their collective mourning a testament to Jane's impact. Vigils were held, candles flickering in the night, each flame a memory, a promise to remember. The bookstore where Jane worked became a makeshift shrine, the windows filled with photos, flowers and notes from those whose lives she touched.

The chilling winds of grief swept through Janice Goldberg's home, not sparing her husband, Jimmy. His once-steady hands now trembled, unable to grasp anything but the weight of loss. Sleep eluded him, replaced by haunting visions of Jane, the daughter they had cherished, the dreams they had woven for her future. Rational thought drowned in the flood of sorrow that engulfed his entire being.

Jimmy's grief was a tempest, shredding the canvas of their existence. Productivity became a distant memory; the mundane tasks of existence lost their significance. The world outside blurred into insignificance; all that mattered was justice for his dear daughter, Jane, and for their shattered family. His heart, once steady, now beat in sync with vengeance.

The authorities became his lifeline with their every move scrutinized, and their diligence demanded. He dialed the police department relentlessly, urging them forward, urging them faster. Jane's killer must be apprehended, tried, convicted, and sentenced. The combative fire within him fueled this relentless pursuit. Sleepless nights blurred into days, and he became a sentinel of grief and rage.

Two weeks after Jane's funeral, a suspect emerged from the shadows. Terrence Taylor, a carpenter, thirty years old, and now etched into their nightmare. Witnesses pointed fingers, their voices trembling. Jane had been seen with him in a white car during an afternoon etched in distress. The car had sped away, leaving her fate hanging in the balance.

And then there was the city prosecutor handling the case—a crusader, they called him. Flamboyant, aggressive, and unyielding. His ambition carved paths through courtrooms, his reputation a double-edged sword. To some, he was a star and a beacon of justice. To others, a pilgarlic, a caricature of excess. His words, like daggers, often pierced the air.

In a prior case, he had declared his goal: convictions, electric chairs. The reporter dared to question the innocents and the price of safety. His reply echoed through the corridors of power: "A few innocents, if it keeps this city safe." A response shocking, audacious, unbecoming a prosecutor and a betrayal of trust. For the public, he was the gatekeeper of justice. But in his flamboyance, perhaps justice itself stood trial.

Terrence Taylor, a carpenter with hands that could shape any wood into art, now felt the cruel craft of fate carving into his very soul. Known in his community for a heart as warm as the hearth he built, Terrence was thrust into a chilling nightmare. The accusation of taking Jane Goldberg's life—a life brimming with promise and vitality—cast a dark pall over his existence. As he stood on the precipice, staring into the abyss of an uncertain future, the scales of justice quivered under the weight of invisible evidence.

The courtroom became an arena where not just Terrence's fate, but the very essence of truth, was on trial. The prosecutor, a man whose ambition was as sharp as the suits he wore, saw Terrence not as a man, but as a rung on the ladder to power. Each headline, each flash of the camera's eye, was a rung on the ladder of his ascent. The governor's chair was the prize, and Terrence's life was but a pawn in the prosecutor's grand design.

In the quiet of his cell, Terrence grappled with the ironies of life. The hands that had once joined wood now joined in prayer, seeking solace in a faith that flickered in the gale of public opinion. His family, a fabric of support, frayed at the edges as the strain of scandal tugged at their bonds. And in the heart of the town, whispers became the wind that swirled around the truth, obscuring it, leaving a community divided and a family clinging to the hope of vindication.

As the trial unfolded, the prosecutor's words painted Terrence not as the man he was, but as a shadow, a specter of fear to be vanquished. And all the while, Terrence's spirit, though besieged by doubt and despair, held onto a single thread of hope—that justice, though blindfolded, would still see the truth.

Before the final verdict was to be delivered, Janice Goldberg found herself in a somber, dimly lit room, face to face with Terrence Taylor— the man whose fate was intertwined with the most painful chapter of her life. The jailhouse, with its cold, unyielding walls, stood as a silent observer to their encounter, a poignant tableau of grief and the search for closure.

Janice, with hands trembling, presented a chronicle of memories captured in photographs—from her daughter's tentative first steps to the vibrant smile that graced her last birthday. Each image was a testament to a life cherished and mourned, a life that Janice held dearer than her own. With a voice choked by emotion, she implored Terrence, seeking just a sliver of truth in the depths of his eyes.

Terrence, with a gravity that belied his years, met her gaze with an unwavering solemnity. "Mother Janice," he began, his voice a whisper of reverence and pain, "I share in the depths of your sorrow, yet I stand before you with a conscience unburdened by the crime attributed to me." His words, carefully chosen, sought not to wound but to convey the sincerity of his innocence.

As Janice absorbed his words, a single tear escaped, tracing a silent path down her cheek—a symbol of the heartache that had become her constant companion. The space between them, filled with the weight of unspoken words and shared anguish, seemed to dissolve as they connected in their mutual loss.

In that moment, the world outside the jailhouse faded into insignificance, and the only truth that mattered was the one they found in each other's presence—a truth that acknowledged the complexity of human emotions and the indelible marks they leave on our souls.

The air was thick with the scent of loss as Janice stepped through the doorway, the familiar creak of the hinges sounding more like a mournful sigh. In the dim light of the living room, she found her husband, a silhouette of sorrow, his gaze lost in the abyss of an unending nightmare. With a voice as fragile as the last leaf of autumn, Janice shared the whispering doubts that fluttered in her heart. "I can't shake the feeling— he's not the one who stole our daughter from us," she breathed, her words trembling in the space between them.

Her husband, once a pillar of strength, now stood fractured by the weight of his despair. Grief had hollowed him out, and rage had set ablaze the remnants of his hope. At her confession, something within him splintered, and his response came as a crackling fire, a tempest of fury and pain. "Don't let his facade deceive you!" he cried out, his voice a shard of glass piercing the quiet. "He's the monster who ended her dreams, her future—our everything!"

In the aftermath of his outburst, a heavy silence fell, a shroud that wrapped around them both. He turned away, his shoulders shaking with the effort to contain the storm within. When he spoke again, it was with a whisper that carried the weight of a thousand unshed tears. "Eternal damnation is too kind for him," he murmured, the words a dark incantation of his longing for justice—or perhaps vengeance. "Nothing less would balance the scales for what he's taken from us."

Janice reached out, her hand trembling as she sought to bridge the chasm of their shared agony. In that moment, they were two souls adrift in a sea of torment, each grappling with the harrowing question: How does one navigate a world that has been irreparably altered by an act of unfathomable cruelty?

And so, in the solemn courtroom, Janice's quivering voice implored the judge, not for herself, but for Terrence. She asked the judge for mercy, not vengeance. The judge listened, moved by her plea. The sentence was thirty-five years in prison, sparing Terrence from death's cold embrace. When asked about her forgiveness, Janice's eyes welled up. "Releasing a burden from my heart," she said. "It's what my Jane would have wanted, compassion over vengeance. Moreover, I am witnessing how the quest for revenge is gradually damaging my husband."

Behind bars, Terrence Taylor found refuge in the pages of textbooks; a lifeline to sanity, a bridge to redemption. Each chapter carried him away from the sterile confines of his cell, closer to a truth he clung to like a fragile promise. "These classes," he'd tell fellow inmates, "aren't mere distractions; they're my path to becoming someone Jane would have believed in."

His letters to Janice, inked with reflections and poetry, traversed the prison walls. Words became stitches, binding their wounds, linking the mother who had lost her daughter, and the man who had lost his freedom. The paper absorbed their shared grief, the ink a silent witness to their unspoken conversations. In his latest letter, he penned a poem that reads:

Forgiveness

In stillness of this place confined,
   With pen in hand, I dwell,
May words that on this page record,
   Be those that pure hearts tell.

Forgiveness is a mighty stream,
  Where God's rich waters flow;
Cleansing the soul, hurt hearts redeem,
  And love's full blossoms grow.

It is the dew that drops on land,
  Where pains and sorrows lay;
Replenishing with fertile ground,
  Of love in full display.

It is the hearts in sorrow draped,
  Yet overcome their gloom;
The graceful ones that love embraced,
  Which in their fullness bloom.

It is the drink that's never laced,
  With bitterness and flaws;
The fare that brings a sweeter taste
  To mouths sullied by hurts.

Mother Janice, your grace shines bright,
  My hope within this grave;
Guiding me through the longest night,
  A gift you freely gave.

And then, there was a glimmer of hope. A dogged, yet doubting officer, haunted by shadows of injustice, reopened the case. DNA testing, which was an elusive technique during Jane's murder investigation, became the beacon. Permissions were secured by him, and a sample from Jane's body embarked on its journey to the lab. Two weeks later, the results arrived, a revelation etched in science.

Buster Cole, an inmate already serving time in prison for another offense, emerged from the shadows. The strands of DNA whispered their secrets; Buster Cole was an almost certain match. Terrence Taylor, who had clung to innocence against a tide of disbelief, even from his own kin, was vindicated. His prior brush with the law, which was a minor traffic violation, paled in comparison to the abyss he had faced.

In a striking coincidence, the true perpetrator, Cole, bore an uncanny resemblance to Taylor: same ethnicity, same towering height, same mustache. And in the annals of tragedy, their white vehicles had intersected. It was a collision of fate and a twist of destiny.

As the prison walls held their secrets, Terrence breathed freedom, a redemption not just for himself, but for Jane, whose memory now danced in the margins of textbooks. And Janice, her heart a montage of forgiveness and grief, whispered to the wind, "Compassion over vengeance."

Upon the emergence of new evidence, a judge's gavel struck the chords of justice, and Terrence Taylor stepped into the light of freedom. The prison gates swung open, releasing him from six years of wrongful imprisonment, a span etched in pain, injustice, and near-death experiences.

On that day of liberation, a reporter, armed with questions, cornered Taylor. The scars from fellow inmates' assaults were still fresh, but his spirit remained unbroken. The reporter probed, relentless, "Do you harbor resentment toward the judicial system?" Taylor's response was a testament to grace: "I forgive them all." But the reporter hungered for more, asking, "How could forgiveness bloom after such darkness?"

Taylor's eyes held memories: the cold bars, the hollow nights. "I've lost six years," he said, "but a mother lost her daughter forever." Jane's absence echoed in his words. Janice's forgiveness, a lifeline, had spared him from the death penalty. Perhaps, in that act of mercy, his own life had been salvaged.

Beneath the vast expanse of an indifferent sky, Janice Goldberg stood—a solitary figure against the stoic backdrop of the prison walls. As Taylor emerged, a free man shackled by the weight of years lost, their embrace was a silent testament to shared grief and unspoken understanding. Janice's apology, a whisper of regret for the injustice he endured, was met with Taylor's quiet fortitude. "God has His plans, and we are but pieces within His vast design," he murmured, his eyes reflecting a soul refined by tribulation, "and through this ordeal, I've found a closeness to God that fills the void where bitterness once festered."

Taylor and Mother Janice left the prison grounds together in Janice's car. As it was now afternoon, Janice decided to stop at the Main Street diner for lunch. While there, she explained to Taylor that her husband, Jimmy, had suffered a stroke on the same day he found out he was wrong about Taylor. He was recuperating in a local hospital. Taylor's response was a gentle wave of compassion, his desire to visit Jimmy not just an offer of consolation, but a silent pledge of forgiveness. Janice, moved by his magnanimity, nodded in agreement, her heart aching with the complexity of emotions that only such a reunion could bring. As they left the diner, the afternoon sun cast long shadows, a reminder that even in the light of new beginnings, the darkness of the past lingers, shaping their lives.

They headed to the hospital room where Jimmy lay on a bed, connected to several intravenous drips. Taylor shook his hand and wished him a speedy recovery. After spending about an hour with Jimmy, just before Janice was to drive Taylor home, Jimmy requested a private word with him. He apologized for not believing in Taylor's innocence, admitting, "My judgment was tainted and imperfect." Taylor understood, sharing that he had lost his mother at a young age to a drug addict's rampage. Janice, moved by his story, wept and lamented Taylor's suffering. After a moment of shared grief, they composed themselves.

Janice drove Taylor home, where they were greeted by a driveway thronged with people, including members of the press. Craving solitude, Taylor courteously asked for privacy and withdrew indoors, bidding Janice goodbye. From that moment on, Taylor and Janice's bond deepened, marked by shared holiday celebrations. Meanwhile, Jimmy's health fully rebounded, and he now relishes fishing excursions and tinkering with cars alongside Taylor. "Their bond is akin to that of father and son," Janice observed, reflecting on the camaraderie between Taylor and her husband. Overcome with emotion, she added, "It's as though I've lost a daughter I hold dear and gained a son who cherishes me in return."

5

Her Reward

In the town of Seguin, Texas, about an hour's drive from San Antonio, Ms. Jackie Wexton served as an elementary school teacher at a Catholic diocese-run school. She embodied the ideal educator—dedicated, intelligent, patient, and deeply invested in her students' welfare. Continuing a family legacy, she was the third generation of educators, following her mother and aunt who taught at elementary and high school levels, respectively. Ms. Wexton embraced innovative teaching methods and earned high regard among her peers. A colleague once lauded her as "a fine head," a nod to both her extensive knowledge and her striking appearance.

With the start of a new school year, each morning brought young Jose Domingo to Ms. Wexton's classroom, his small frame often shrouded in a cloud of sadness and tears. His clothes, a size too small, clung to him like remnants of a life that was struggling to keep up with his growth. Despite his disheveled appearance and the disorientation that seemed to set him apart from his peers, there was an undeniable charm to Jose. His eyes, when not clouded by sorrow, shone with a brightness that hinted at a lively spirit, and his build, though slight, suggested a resilience waiting to be uncovered. Yet, these glimpses of the boy he could be were often eclipsed by the distress that seemed to envelop him.

Ms. Wexton, with years of experience etched into her compassionate demeanor, initially mistook Jose's quietude for the sullenness that sometimes accompanies the adjustment to a new environment. However, as the days turned into weeks, it became apparent that Jose's struggles ran deeper than mere reluctance. He lagged behind his classmates, not for lack of intelligence, but because an unseen burden tethered him to a place of desolation.

Driven by a blend of concern and curiosity, Ms. Wexton turned to a method that had never failed her—the universal language of kindness expressed through food. One day, she reached into her lunch bag and retrieved a cookie, the kind that makes a child's eyes light up with delight. "I was saving this for Linda," she thought aloud, "but perhaps Jose needs it more." Handing the cookie to Jose, she watched as he consumed it with a fervor that spoke volumes of the hunger that had been gnawing at him, both physically and emotionally.

The cookie, though a small gesture, became a bridge between them. It was an offering that transcended the mere quelling of hunger; it was an acknowledgment of his existence, a sign that he was seen and that he mattered. Later that day, during a quiet moment, Ms. Wexton approached Jose, who now seemed a touch lighter, a bit more present. With gentle words, she invited him to share the worries that lay heavy on his heart.

As Jose opened up, revealing the tangled web of challenges he faced at home, Ms. Wexton listened with a heart that understood the language of unspoken pain. Together, they began to unravel the threads of his troubles, each conversation a step towards the light of hope and the promise of a future where his smiles would no longer be rare, but a radiant testament to the strength of the human spirit.

"My parents are gone, so I shuttle between my two aunts. When one grows weary of my presence, she sends me to the other on the bus," the little boy confided, his voice a soft echo of resignation. Ms. Wexton, caught in the raw honesty of Jose's words, felt a poignant blend of sorrow and shock ripple through her. A surge of protective anger welled up within her towards the aunts, a fierce mama bear instinct awakened.

She resolved then and there to bridge the gap of indifference. At the meeting, her voice trembled with restrained emotion as she laid bare the aunts' neglect, her words a scathing rebuke to their callous disregard for a child so vulnerable. With a steely gaze, she warned of the impending storm—the involvement of Child Protective Services— should they fail to rewrite the narrative of Jose's care.

Later on, Jose began to excel in many subjects, particularly the sciences— biology, chemistry, and physics—and overall academic performance, under the watchful eye of his newfound mother figure, Ms. Wexton. She ensured her classroom was always stocked with various snacks for Jose and his classmates and continued to follow up on Jose's progress even after he moved on from her class. As a result, Jose graduated from high school and proceeded to college, carrying with him the enduring memory of Ms. Wexton's love, care, and attention.

A quarter-century had composed its medley, and Ms. Wexton, now cradling the wisdom of 65 years, stood at a precipice. The diagnosis was a thunderclap in clear skies: a large brain tumor, a silent usurper lurking within. Surgeons, those maestros of the scalpel, each echoed the same somber refrain—the promise of a cure was a flickering candle in the wind, dimmed by the tumor's audacious sprawl and the peril it posed to the delicate symphony of her nerves.

In this labyrinth of uncertainty, a beacon emerged: Dr. Jose Jesus Domingo. The very name was a melody from the past, a reminder of a young boy whose potential she had tenderly fostered. The day she crossed the threshold of his office, time folded upon itself. Their embrace was an ocean of shared history, each tear a pearl of gratitude and hope. She saw in him the boy she once knew, his spirit now housed in the assured presence of a healer.

In the sanctuary of his office, Ms. Wexton's family encircled her, a living testament to her legacy. Dr. Domingo, once a seedling in her academic garden, now stood among them, a towering oak. The reunion was a collage of emotion—pride, joy, and an unspoken understanding that transcended bloodlines. "We are all one family," the words resonated, a chorus of unity that had its roots in the classroom where Ms. Wexton had sown the seeds of community and compassion. It was a mantra that had blossomed in Jose's heart, and now, it was his turn to nurture her, to repay the gift of growth she had given him.

In the days leading up to the surgery, Dr. Domingo was a bundle of confidence and nerves. Sleep eluded him, not from doubt in his abilities, but from the weight of gratitude. He was about to operate on Ms. Wexton, the very person whose kindness had once steered his life to safer shores. In quiet moments, he would recite a prayer from a book—a treasured gift from Ms. Wexton herself. The words were a balm to his restless spirit: "O God, all good gifts come from You. Grant us the power to recognize that our talents and all that we possess are but loans from Your bounty. May we use these gifts in alignment with Your will."

On the morning of the surgery, Ms. Wexton's confidence was palpable, her composure unmarred by uhtceare—a pre-dawn anxiety. As Dr. Domingo, alongside his team of skilled doctors and nurses, navigated the complexities of the procedure, they encountered numerous challenges.

Yet, each was surmounted with the precision and foresight of their extensive training. Their confidence never wavered, bolstered by the belief that their preparation would lead to a successful outcome.

The surgery concluded with unexpected smoothness, and following a period of rehabilitation, Ms. Wexton was poised to resume her everyday life. In a gesture of heartfelt celebration, Dr. Domingo rallied the hospital staff to serenade Ms. Wexton. Her recovery room, adorned with an abundance of flowers, ribbons, balloons, and heartfelt wishes for wellness, echoed with melodies of hope and joy.

Dr. Domingo read a poem he penned to Ms. Wexton:

A Mother's Love

A mother's love is matchless;
    In a world with no peer,
Its gifts are pure and endless,
    In you, it's been quite clear.

The nature of your passion,
    Mere words cannot describe,
No one loves in such fashion;
    Only to you ascribe.

Your love's cast with compassion,
    Compelling it to love,
E'en more the adaptation,
    Of those it loves to live.

In every trial and testing,
    Your love stands firm and true;
A beacon ever resting,
    On shores of life anew.

Your love brings satisfaction,
     To those it has transformed;
There's hush of expectation
     On rewards it has stored.

Thank God for you, dear mother;
     The many souls you've touched,
Whose lives are rich and better,
     Only because you cared.

With a voice softened by the passage of years, Dr. Domingo unfurled the tale of a simple cookie—a morsel that became the cornerstone of his destiny. He spoke of Ms. Wexton, a beacon of hope in his turbulent childhood, whose unwavering dedication had steered him away from the precipice of despair. The conversation that she had with his aunt, a moment etched in the annals of his memory, was a catalyst that reshaped his world.

He pondered, with a heart brimming with introspection, whether it was the looming shadow of Child Protective Services or the genuine concern in Ms. Wexton's eyes that touched the core of his aunt's being. The transformation was profound; her once-stern gaze softened, her words, once sharp as thorns, now carried the gentle cadence of affection.

From that pivotal day, the warmth of his aunt's newfound kindness enveloped him, nurturing his wounded spirit. Dr. Domingo's gratitude was a river that flowed deep and true, for the change that blossomed within his family's heart was the very essence of his salvation.

In a twist of serendipity, Dr. Domingo's aunt graced the hospital corridors, her arrival as unexpected as a summer rain. Though her visits were a consistent theme in the story of his life, today, her presence was a gift unannounced. She had been the matriarchal anchor in his tempestuous youth, and now, he introduced her with a tender reverence to those gathered as the aunt of his storied past.

The staff's reactions painted a mosaic of human emotion, a canvas of curiosity and understanding. Side by side with the nurses, Dr. Domingo led her through the quiet halls to Ms. Wexton's sanctuary. With a gentle inquiry, he bridged the years between them, "Do you recognize this remarkable woman?" Recognition dawned in his aunt's eyes, a mirror to a moment long past, when Ms. Wexton stood as a guardian of hope.

What followed was an embrace that spoke volumes, a circle of arms that drew together the threads of their shared history. Laughter bubbled forth, pure and unguarded, as lemonade and snacks passed from hand to hand, symbols of a simple yet profound communion. His aunt, with a voice rich with emotion, offered her thanks to Ms. Wexton, not just for her steadfast love and concern, but for the grace she extended to a family once fractured.

Ms. Wexton, ever the humble steward of her calling, deflected the praise. She spoke of duty, not as an obligation, but as a privilege—the privilege of nurturing young lives, of standing firm for the voiceless, and of kindling the potential within each child. Her words were a testament to the belief that every adult bears the torch of advocacy for the young, a torch that illuminates the path to a brighter future.

Ms. Wexton stood before the assembly, her voice resonating with a warmth that wrapped around each listener like a comforting embrace. "Indeed," she began, her eyes sweeping across the sea of faces, "countless souls across our vast world dedicate themselves daily to molding the futures of our young ones. This noble circle includes not only parents and guardians but also educators, healthcare workers, spiritual guides, counselors, volunteers, and even those within our own families."

She spoke of the silent heroes who toil in the shadows, their actions often unnoticed by the masses, yet whose impact ripples through the structural web that underpins society's collective existence. "They are the unsung, propelled not by the desire for recognition, but by a deep-seated conviction, professional dedication, or perhaps a whisper of divine inspiration," she said, her voice tinged with emotion.

As Ms. Wexton continued, her words painted a picture of selfless service, of lives touched and transformed by acts of kindness and wisdom. "While the world may overlook their contributions, the true measure of their worth may transcend this earthly realm. Some find their compensation in material form, but others, like myself, we find our riches in the indelible marks we leave on the hearts and minds we touch."

The room grew still, the air thick with introspection as her message sank deep. "So, when fate presents you with the opportunity to shape a life, seize it with both hands. Infuse it with positivity, for such an act has the power to echo back into your own life in ways unimaginable."

Her closing words hung in the air, a poignant reminder of the interconnectedness of our lives. The room erupted in a chorus of affirmations, a symphony of shared understanding and commitment. And as they embraced, the atmosphere was charged with a profound sense of unity and purpose.

In a twist that seemed almost fated, a teacher who had reached out to save her student found herself rescued in return. It was a testament to the transformative power of giving, a reminder that in the act of saving another, we may very well be saving ourselves.

After her surgery, Ms. Wexton spent some time in rehabilitation, and Dr. Domingo made sure to keep tabs on her progress. His interest in Ms. Wexton's wellbeing extended beyond professional courtesy; he was now dating her youngest daughter, Julia, and their relationship was becoming serious. They had eyed each other since the first time she walked into his office with her mum. Before meeting him, Julia's romantic endeavors were less than fortunate. Her first love, Jason, was a ne'er-do-well. Despite her efforts, their relationship floundered. Unmotivated and lackluster, he was the antithesis of the hardworking, focused, and affectionate Julia.

Ms. Wexton once likened him to a legless chair that Julia attempted to support with sticks and duct tape—a relationship doomed to fail, as she had predicted.

Julia's subsequent relationship also ended in disappointment when she discovered that Theodore, her then-boyfriend, was unfaithful. One evening, she walked into his apartment to find him inebriated and in compromising circumstances with two other women. This incident terminated their brief and tumultuous relationship, leaving Julia's hopes for love severely jaded. She closed her heart to romantic pursuits, likening it to a sealed, impenetrable metal gate.

Dr. Domingo, however, was a stark contrast to her past experiences. He cherished her, providing the love and attention for which she had longed. The couple devoted time to each other, engaging in typical activities like walks and dinners, as well as fulfilling Julia's childhood dream of traveling to Disney World, exploring the West Coast, and touring Eastern Europe.

A year into their nascent relationship, on a bright, sunny Saturday afternoon at the Wexton residence with the air tingling with anticipation, the couple, Jose and Julia, stood before their families, hearts brimming with joy. They joyfully announced their engagement to their families, with plans to marry. The news moved Ms. Wexton to tears, and even Mr. Wexton, who had been privy to the secret, couldn't help but become emotional. Dr. Domingo's aunt and other relatives were also present to share in the celebration.

Following a year of courtship, Jose and Julia exchanged vows in a quaint local church, surrounded by their loved ones. After their heartfelt vows, Jose and Julia stepped into a vibrant banquet hall adorned with twinkle lights and the promise of celebration. The air hummed with anticipation as guests gathered, their smiles echoing the couple's joy.

Bands played, their melodies weaving through the room—a symphony of love and shared dreams. The parquet dance floor beckoned, and Jose and Julia swirled—a waltz of promises kept, of futures knotted. Friends and family cheered, their laughter punctuating the music.

The banquet hall overflowed with life—tables laden with delicacies, glasses raised in toasts. And as the night unfolded, Jose whispered to Julia, "This is our beginning—a dance of forever." She nodded, her eyes reflecting the stars above—their love story etched in every note, every step.

Now, as husband and wife, they reside contentedly in Houston, a city that cradles their memories and their shared laughter. Dr. Domingo's new practice thrives, while Julia's classroom echoes with the sounds of curiosity and learning. Together, they raise a young child—a testament to love's resilience, to second chances.

And in quiet moments, when the band's melodies fade, they hold hands—a promise renewed, a lifetime unfolding.

Ms. Wexton and her husband make regular visits to cherish time with their grandchild, and each time, grandma brings some cookies for her little one. Sometimes, Jose, the father, watches in admiration as grandma feeds cookies to his child, recalling memories of his own childhood, savoring cookies in Ms. Wexton's classroom.

On sunny weekends, the family gathers in the park, where laughter mingles with the rustling leaves. Dr. Domingo pushes the swing gently, sending peals of joy into the air. Julia watches over, her heart full, as the generations blend seamlessly, the past and the present dancing in harmony. Their home, once quiet, now brims with life—each room tells a story, each picture on the wall smiles back with the joy of shared moments.

As the city lights twinkle in the twilight, they tuck their child into bed, whispering tales of dreams and adventure. Houston, not just a city, but a canvas of their love, holds them close, nurturing their hopes for the future.

6

His Mountain

In 2010, Charles Johnson, affectionately known as "Chuck" to his friends and family, embarked on a new chapter in Nevada with his wife, Judy, and son, Joshua. Chuck joined a tech company as a senior engineer, while Judy became a manager at a local bank. The family settled in the charming town of Lamoille, nestled at the base of the majestic Ruby Mountains. Lamoille, with its quaint streets lined with mom-and-pop shops, exudes a warmth that extends beyond its sunny summers. The town's heart beats in the central square, where festivals and farmers' markets brim with local produce and artisanal crafts. As autumn unfurls, Lamoille is set ablaze with fiery hues, with the Ruby Mountains standing sentinel as leaves dance to the ground. Winter cloaks the town in serene whites, and the crisp air is filled with the laughter of children sledding down gentle slopes. Come spring, the valleys are a symphony of blooming wildflowers, and the mountains' melting snow feeds crystal-clear streams that meander through the landscape. This idyllic setting is not just a feast for the eyes but a balm for the soul, offering a tranquil retreat from the bustle of city life. Chuck, Judy, and Joshua found more than a home in Lamoille; they found a community where life's simple pleasures are cherished, and the beauty of nature is revered.

Chuck, a towering figure of intellect and kindness, quickly became a cornerstone in his workplace and community. His knack for innovation and problem-solving made him an invaluable asset, and his unwavering ethical compass guided his interactions, earning him the respect and admiration of colleagues and newcomers alike. His mentorship was likened to that of a sage, with one junior engineer fondly comparing him to the biblical Job, a symbol of patience, faithfulness, and resilience.

The Johnsons' residence was a mere mile from the Ruby Mountains, an imposing range that spanned eleven miles in width and soared to heights of approximately 11,000 feet. The mountains, a natural wonder, became a sanctuary for Chuck and the townspeople, who would venture towards its base to bask in its splendor or partake in a rejuvenating jog or walk.

Five years into his tenure, Chuck aspired to ascend the corporate ladder, driven by a belief that he could spearhead change and better actualize his innovative visions. Despite his extensive qualifications and dedication, the elusive promotion remained out of reach, with less experienced peers often surpassing him. Even when a protégé, whom he had mentored, advanced due to social connections, Chuck's resolve did not waver. He sought constructive feedback and strived for self-improvement, yet the managerial role remained just beyond his grasp.

Disheartened but not defeated, Chuck shifted his focus to the world outside the office walls. He often wrote poems, volunteered at his son's school, participated in the town's leadership council, and found solace in the arms of nature, embracing evening strolls to the mountain's base as a newfound passion. With each step, he uncovered more of the mountain's secrets, its towering presence a stark contrast to the distant view he once knew. The Ruby Mountains stood as a testament to nature's grandeur, their peaks reaching skyward, etched against the canvas of the Nevada sky. Their beauty was a balm to Chuck's spirit, a reminder of the enduring strength and serenity that lay in the heart of the earth.

Months of walking to the mountain's base had filled Chuck with a sense of curiosity and a touch of restlessness. The Ruby Mountains, once a symbol of beauty and a shield against the elements, now stood as a barrier to the unseen world beyond. He pondered the view from the summit and the hidden landscapes on the other side. He thought about a possible helicopter ride but dismissed the idea. Each visit to the mountain seemed to echo with an invitation, a challenge from the mountain itself: "Why don't you find out?"

Yielding to this call, Chuck, alongside his family, ventured eastward around the Ruby Mountains on a crisp autumn afternoon. The journey unfolded as a gallery of nature's artistry, with the wind choreographing a dance of fiery leaves under a cloudless sky. However, the reality that awaited on the other side was a stark contrast to their expectations. The relics of a past mining epoch loomed as mute guardians over the barren landscape, a far cry from the lush vistas of Lamoille. These towering structures, once the heartbeat of a thriving industry, now lay abandoned, their rusted frameworks overtaken by the relentless march of nature. The air hung heavy with the scent of pine and earth, a stark contrast to the acrid tang of metal and sweat that once permeated the area. Where laughter and camaraderie had echoed against the stone, there was now only the whisper of the wind through the pines, carrying with it the faintest hints of stories untold. The ground, littered with relics of the past, bore the scars of excavation, a testament to the human endeavor that had once sought to wrest treasures from its depths. Yet, in this quiet decay, there was a sense of profound peace, as if the land had finally reclaimed what was always meant to be wild and free.

The revelation was a bitter pill for Chuck, but it was Judy's insight the following evening that began to mend his disillusionment. She illuminated the wonders that Chuck had overlooked: the wildlife that adorned the mountainside, the flora that painted it with life, and the symphony of birds, insects, and the whispering trees. It was a world that Chuck, ever the problem-solver, had neglected in his pursuit of what lay beyond.

On his subsequent solitary trek, as he paused to embrace the splendor his wife had revealed, the mountain seemed to question him with a knowing whisper, "Not as green on the other side?" No words were spoken in reply, yet the mountain's query resonated within him. It was a moment of clarity, an understanding that sometimes, the beauty and value of what is present outweigh the allure of change and the unknown.

A vacancy at work and a successful bid for a managerial position made Chuck a manager at last. His journey to management was a testament to his perseverance and fairness. His equitable treatment of colleagues earned him not just a managerial position but also the affection and respect of those around him.

After three years as a manager, the office head organized a gathering for the managerial team at a resort in Arizona. Chuck brought his laptop and work materials, anticipating a business-oriented trip. However, it turned out to be a retreat—a common practice by the office head for managers to unwind and rejuvenate. Upon arrival, Chuck inquired about the agenda for work-related activities to organize his tasks. The office head assured him that it wasn't necessary. On the initial day, the managers primarily engaged in leisurely dining and socializing by the Lazy River. Chuck considered this an inefficient use of time and company assets, yet he chose not to voice his concerns. Subsequently, the managers decided to visit a club, but Chuck opted out, remaining outside to wait for his colleagues.

The retreat in Arizona, however, presented a moral quandary. The frivolity of the lazy river and the unexpected visit to a gentleman's club were at odds with Chuck's values. His decision to remain outside, to maintain his integrity, was a silent act of defiance against the indulgence he witnessed.

Upon returning to his hotel, Chuck's conversation with Judy highlighted the strength of their bond and her unwavering trust in his character. Yet, the weight of the situation lingered. The misuse of company funds and the potential damage to his reputation haunted him. Alone in his room, Chuck grappled with the conflict between his ethical standards and the loyalty expected by his peers. It was a crossroads moment, one that would define his path forward and the legacy he would leave behind.

One month later, a complaint was lodged against Joseph Paterson, a manager, by Marian Fluton, a bright young lady, who graduated from a top university, alleging that he had harassed her during a trip to Massachusetts. Paterson denied the allegations to Human Resources (HR) personnel, yet admitted to his fellow managers during a meeting that he had kissed and groped her without her consent while in a drunken stupor, but claimed he did not intend to harass her.

Chuck watched as his peers navigated the fallout with casual indifference that chilled him to the bone. He found himself at a crossroads. His HR interview loomed ahead. The other managers had played their cards well, weaving a web of half-truths during their interviews. They reveled in their cunning, protecting one of their own, who had crossed ethical boundaries.

As Chuck sat at his desk, restless and conflicted, his colleagues whispered reminders: "Be a team player," they urged. "Cover for him. After all, the victim is just a young engineer, lower in rank." The pressure mounted, and Chuck felt the weight of loyalty tugging at his conscience.

That evening, Chuck laced up his running shoes and headed out for a jog. His destination? His favorite spot to clear his mind, Ruby Mountains. But as he ran, he couldn't escape the voice that echoed in his mind—a voice that wasn't his own.

"So, you're going to cave?" Ruby's words cut through the mental fog. Ignoring Ruby wasn't easy. A couple of times, Chuck muttered, "No, I'm not," but the conviction wavered. Ruby persisted. "But it did cross your mind, didn't it?" Chuck hesitated, then admitted, "Yes, it did."

Ruby's tone turned adamant. "There's nothing to think about here." The words hung heavy. "That young woman could have been your daughter or sister. She looked to you as a protector, a shield from predators."

Chuck frowned. Ruby continued, "In the same way, Lamoille looks to me for protection from nature's elements. I exist for a purpose, placed here by forces higher than us. Would you be fine if I stood by and let the next storm destroy Lamoille? Or failed to capture snow in winter, denying it fresh water in summer?"

The analogy struck Chuck. Lamoille depended on Ruby's watchful eye. And Suzie, his niece who'd recently graduated from college, depended on people like him. What if she faced abuse from a superior at work? Chuck's resolve hardened. He couldn't betray his principles, even if it meant alienating friends.

As the moon rose on his way back home, Chuck whispered to the invisible presence beside him, "I get it now, Ruby. I won't be silent. Not this time."

And so, the next day, when HR asked about the incident, Chuck spoke truthfully. The web of deceit unraveled, and the young engineer found justice. In his colleagues' judgment, his act was worse than treason.

His peers, ensnared in a web of half-truths and self-preservation, could not understand Chuck's stoicism. To them, the office was a chessboard, and every move was a gambit for personal gain. But Chuck saw beyond the immediate horizon. His stance, though isolating, became a beacon of integrity in a murky ethical landscape. It was a declaration that some lines should never be crossed, that the end does not always justify the means.

In the weeks that followed, Chuck's isolation became more pronounced. Whispers turned into outright avoidance, and the once warm greetings now gave way to cold shoulders. Yet, through it all, Chuck remained undeterred. He knew that integrity was not a commodity to be traded but a cornerstone of one's character. As the office dynamics continued to unravel, Chuck's reputation as a man of principle only grew stronger. It was a lonely path, but for Chuck, it was the only one worth walking. On a dusky evening, with the weight of injustice from work heavy on his mind, Chuck trudged along the path toward The Ruby Mountains, his heart heavy with disappointment. The job he had pursued relentlessly, the view from the mountaintop he had envisioned, all fell short of his expectations. The summit, once a beacon of achievement, now seemed lackluster.

Arriving at Ruby's base, Chuck sank onto a weathered bench. Birds flitted around him, squabbling over tossed peanuts and crumbs. Their petty battles mirrored the complexities of human existence. But today, Chuck wasn't in the mood for avian drama.

And then, as if summoned by his thoughts, Ruby's voice whispered in his mind: "Lonely at the top?"

Chuck sighed. "Not now, Ruby," he muttered. "I'm not in the mood."

But Ruby persisted. "Cheer up. You did the right thing."

Chuck glanced around, then closed his eyes and listened.

Ruby's words flowed like a gentle stream. "You've often wondered what my summit looks like." Chuck nodded, curious despite himself.

Ruby continued, "The trees on my peak—they've stood there for centuries. Strong, determined, weathering every storm. They protect what's around and below, silently fulfilling their purpose."

Chuck frowned. "But do they ever feel weary? After all, storms can be relentless."

Ruby's voice grew more animated. "Ah, my friend, that's the beauty of it. You see, those trees never mope. They don't lament their fate. Why? Because they find satisfaction in knowing they've likely saved generations of people, plants, and animals."

Chuck absorbed the wisdom. "Satisfaction," he repeated. "That's what keeps them going."

Ruby chuckled. "Exactly. It's all they've got—the knowledge that they matter. And you, Chuck, have climbed your own mountain."

Chuck blinked. "I have?"

Ruby's tone turned firm. "Yes. You stood up for what's right, even when it meant alienating friends. That young engineer—the victim—she could've been your daughter or sister. She could have been Suzie. You shielded her. Be proud of that."

As Chuck walked back home, he replayed his discourse with Ruby, his moral compass, urging him toward integrity. And now, Chuck was reassured. He'd done right, just like those ancient trees atop Ruby Mountains.

After a talk with his wife, Judy, Chuck tendered his resignation, but not before sending a letter to their head office in California about the toxic culture of the office in Lamoille. He landed a new job as a manager at a tech firm, where he has successfully trained and mentored many engineers.

In the end, Chuck's decision to resign and expose the office's toxic culture was his ascent to a personal summit. He realized that the most significant peaks to conquer were not those of the Ruby Mountains but the ethical heights he achieved through his actions. His subsequent success at a new company and the positive changes that ensued at his former workplace affirmed the value of his choices.

Chuck's walks to the Ruby Mountains have since taken on a new meaning. No longer seeking answers or yearning for unseen vistas, he finds contentment in the beauty and strength that surrounds him. The mountains, in their silent wisdom, no longer pose questions, for they recognize a man at peace with his path and the world he has helped shape.

He wrote a poem about life's mountains which reads:

Life's Mountains

Mountains of life are faced each day,
    By all with will to rise,
Above impediments that may,
    Along their paths arise.

Life's mountain more than stone and earth,
    A fate carved with each step;
A show of will, a test of worth,
    For all who dare to hope.

Each ledge, a careful step to face,
    Those winds with struggles laced.
A noble mind will e'er efface,
    The strife that life encased.

The slopes are steep, the valleys deep,
    We find with each ascent,
And dreams may falter, sorrows seep,
    Yet, climb e'en when we're spent.

We scale seasons of sun and strife,
    Each ledge a lesson learned.
Its peaks with much delight are rife,
    For triumph over brood.

Trek on with courage in each heart,
    Hope for our journey's best,
Our truest selves, each climb impart,
    With souls set free at last.

After Chuck left his old firm, he encountered a former colleague at a grocery store one Saturday afternoon. The colleague subtly hinted that Chuck's departure had cost him a significant promotion at the Lamoille office, suggesting that assimilation into the office culture was a prerequisite for advancement. Chuck, however, stood firm in his belief that maintaining high ethical standards was paramount, regardless of the prevailing office culture. He argued that integrity should not be compromised for professional gain, and that ethical conduct was essential for building a respectful and trustworthy work environment.

Chuck's stance serves as a reminder that ethical integrity can carry more weight than hierarchical success, and that sometimes, standing by one's principles is the true mark of leadership.

7

Jealousy, Poison of My Heart

"Dr. Smith, line 2, Dr. Smith, line 2, please." The Detroit, Michigan hospital intercom crackled urgently, pulling Dr. David Smith from his focused concentration in the operating room. His gloved hands hovered over the patient's chest, the scalpel poised mid-air. The sterile lights glinted off his glasses as he turned toward the speaker.

"Dr. Smith, line 2, please," the voice repeated, urgency lacing every syllable. The Operating Room nurse glanced at him, concern etching her features. Dr. Smith nodded, his heart pounding. It wasn't every day that a surgeon received a page like this.

He stepped out of the operating theater, the door swinging shut behind him. The corridor was a blur of white walls and fluorescent lights. His mind raced through the possibilities. Had there been a complication? A critical case? He couldn't afford to lose focus; lives depended on him.

But when he reached the nurses' station, it wasn't a medical emergency awaiting him. Instead, the receptionist handed him the phone, her eyes sympathetic. "It's your mother," she whispered.

Dr. Smith's breath caught. His mother—seriously ill? The news hit him like a sledgehammer. He hadn't seen her since he left home at seventeen, chasing his dreams of becoming a surgeon. Guilt gnawed at him; he'd missed birthdays, holidays, and countless moments that could never be reclaimed.

He took the receiver, his hand trembling. "Hello?" His voice cracked, betraying the turmoil within.

"David," her voice was frail, but unmistakably his mother's. "It's me. I don't have much time."

He sank into the nearest chair, the sterile hospital scent mixing with memories of home-cooked meals and bedtime stories. "Mom," he whispered. "Come home. Please," she said.

He hung up, the phone slipping from his grasp. His mind raced. He'd leave work, catch the next flight. But what awaited him there? A mother he barely knew anymore?

His wife, Mary, found him packing his bags at home. She didn't ask questions, just held him as he wept silently. "You have to go," she said. "She's your mother."

And so, Dr. David Smith left home for Pennsylvania. The plane ride was a blur, the miles stretching like an eternity. Throughout the night, he lay awake, staring at the cabin ceiling, wondering how he'd face the woman who'd given him life.

But Mary's words echoed in his mind: "All will be well." He clung to that promise, praying it would hold true.

The next day, Dr. David Smith arrived at the dimly lit hospital room in Pennsylvania. The sterile scent of antiseptic clung to the air, mingling with memories of childhood—a time when he'd run through sun-dappled fields, his mother's laughter echoing behind him. But those memories were distant now, buried beneath years of hurt and absence.

His mother lay there, frail and fragile, her once-vibrant eyes now dulled by illness. As he extended his hand toward her, recognition dawned. Tears welled in her eyes, and she reached for him, wrapping an arm around his shoulders. The touch was tentative, as if afraid he might vanish like a mirage.

"David," she whispered, her voice trembling. "My son."

He swallowed the lump in his throat. The room seemed to hold its breath, waiting for the reunion that had been denied for too long. Overwhelmed with gratitude, she clung to him, her body quivering with the contact. It was as if his presence filled the room with an inexplicable brightness, pushing back the shadows of regret.

"Why haven't you come home to visit, my son?" Her voice cracked, and she wiped tears from her cheeks. "Why all these years?"

His anger surged, a tempest threatening to consume him. He'd rehearsed this moment—the confrontation, the catharsis—but now that it was here, words failed him. He met her gaze, the pain etched in her features. The years of longing, of unanswered questions, hung heavy between them.

"Joshua," he spat out the name. "Your favorite."

Her eyes widened, and she shook her head. "David, I—"

"Don't," he interrupted. "Don't pretend it didn't happen. When I needed help with homework, you barely spared a moment for me. John, my older brother, became my tutor. And Joshua? You paid for his camping trips, claiming there wasn't enough money for mine. The countless times he had free rein, while John and I were confined by your strict rules."

His voice trembled with suppressed rage. "When I left for college, I vowed never to return. To build my own life, start my own family. To treat my children better than you treated me."

His mother's face crumpled. "David, I—"

At that moment, David's voice echoed down the hospital hallway. Consumed by anger, he didn't pause to inquire about her well-being. He wanted her to feel remorse for her shortcomings, real or perceived, to experience the pain he believed she had inflicted upon him.

At this pivotal moment, David's mother clung to his hands as if they were a lifeline. Her grip tightened, and her breaths slowed, each one a fragile thread connecting her to life. The room seemed to hold its breath, cocooned in the weight of their shared history.

"My son," she began, her voice trembling like a fragile leaf in the wind. "After your father passed away, things became impossibly hard for me." Her eyes, once vibrant, now held the weariness of years. "On some days, when I pretended to go to my job, I was actually at Uncle Ken's small store, helping out for a few dollars." She paused, her gaze searching his face. "I'd lost my job when the factory shut down."

David's anger flared. His voice, belligerent, sliced through the air. "But you never said a word to us."

"Yes," she admitted, her fingers tracing the lines etched on his palm. "I didn't want you, my children, to worry. You see, your little brother Joshua wasn't a normal child." Her eyes flickered with memories—of late nights poring over textbooks, of therapy sessions, of fierce determination. "He had learning disabilities, but I was determined not to let that change anything. I wanted him to have a life as normal as any other child's."

David's mind raced. Joshua, the brother he'd resented, the one who'd always been the golden child. "That's why you devoted so much time to his development," he said, bitterness tainting his words.

"You and your older brother were fine," she continued, her voice a fragile thread. "But Joshua needed more. He struggled to remember things he learned. His world was a puzzle, and I was determined to help him piece it together."

"Is that why he was doing poorly in school?" David's voice cracked. The wounds of childhood reopened, raw and bleeding.

"Yes," his mother replied. "His grades didn't reflect his effort. But I was lenient with him because he wasn't like you. You were normal, and he was not." Her gaze held his, unflinching. "You should be proud of your brother. He talks about you all the time. He works at the Elmwood Zoo in Norristown."

The room seemed to exhale, releasing years of hurt and misunderstanding. David's anger wavered, replaced by a maelstrom of emotions. Could forgiveness bridge the chasm that separated them? Could he let go of the seventeen-year-old boy who'd vowed never to return home?

As he looked into his mother's eyes, he realized that healing might be possible. And perhaps, just perhaps, love could find its way back into their fractured hearts.

A few minutes later, John, the eldest brother, appeared in the hospital room. Behind him, a frantic Joshua, the zookeeper, who couldn't contain his excitement at seeing his brother David. He burst into the room, screaming loudly and pacing like a child in a candy store. Tears streamed down his face as he hugged David, pouring out his love and longing. "Why did you stay away?" Joshua's voice trembled with emotion, but David remained silent.

After the emotional meeting, Joshua extended an invitation to David. Reluctantly, David accepted and found himself at Joshua's house just outside of Norristown. The air was thick with memories and unspoken words. As Joshua called out to his wife, "Honey, my brother is here; come and meet him," David's eyes scanned the room.

And there it was—a large picture of himself, his wife, and their two children, prominently displayed at the center of the family room. Below it, photos of his other brother, John, and his children formed a collage of family ties. David's heart tightened. "How did you get my pictures?" he asked, his voice tight.

"From the internet," Joshua replied, unabashed. "Your hospital brochures. I printed them and had them framed."

As they talked, children's voices echoed from outside. Joshua's kids were returning from school. He called out, "David, bring your sister here to meet your uncle."

"His name is David?" The elder David raised an eyebrow.

"Yes," Joshua beamed. "I named him after you, his uncle. Guess what? He's bright and is going to be a doctor, just like you."

The room blurred as tears welled up. David's emotions surged; a mix of regret, forgiveness, and overwhelming love. He wept uncontrollably, and Joshua and his wife tried to console him. In that moment, surrounded by family, David realized that healing was possible, and perhaps, just perhaps, he could find his way back home.

As Joshua left the room to attend to his children, his wife leaned in closer to David. Her eyes held a mixture of warmth and sadness. "My husband," she confided, "speaks of you incessantly. He wishes he were you, so he could help the sick animals at the zoo." Her voice trembled, as if revealing a secret long held. "Whenever he called and couldn't reach you, he'd tell me the hospital staff said you were terribly busy with patients. But he was certain you'd call back someday."

David's heart clenched. Joshua—the brother he'd resented—had carried his memory like a beacon. "What about his disabilities?" David asked, his voice softer now.

"Some days are better than others," she replied. "He remembers certain things but forgets others. But one thing is for sure: he never forgot you." She smiled, a bittersweet expression. "He boasts about you to everyone at church and in our community. He genuinely loves and admires you."

David's composure wavered. Jealousy, like a poison, had tainted their relationship for years. He'd missed out on the simple joy of being loved unconditionally. Alone one night, he'd faced the mirror of his own foolishness. The seventeen-year-old boy who'd vowed never to return home had grown into a man burdened by regret.

And so, in that quiet room, surrounded by memories and the scent of antiseptic, Dr. David Smith began to heal. He whispered his remorse to the walls, hoping they'd carry it to the heavens. Perhaps forgiveness was possible. Perhaps love could mend what time had fractured.

And as he wept, he realized that sometimes, the greatest healing came from the most unexpected places—like a brother who loved animals and a mother who'd sacrificed silently. He reflected on his foolishness toward his family and expressed his remorse in a poem about jealousy that he wrote:

Jealousy

Jealousy, poison of my heart;
    That I should treasure not my gifts
But yearn that not of me a part,
    While cruelty invade my thoughts.

My heart indifferent to their needs,
    Despite their many noble deeds
And oft begrudges what it sees,
    Although with means that ne'er recedes.

Jealousy, you find faults that aren't;
    Monster mocking meal it feeds on,
With biased brush, others you paint,
    Although their hearts are pure within.

You delight in the spites of man
    With a quite sickening, jolly sense.
Hence, my once foolish mind will ban!
    Spare me, this vile moral offense.

Jealousy, fragrance of frayed hearts
    From flowers grown on sullied soil,
Your stench will end when man departs
    From those desires his soil despoil.

Their mother, after several months of rehabilitation at the hospital, returned home and is doing quite well, happy that her sons are back together. While at the hospital, Dr. David Smith inquired about possible vacancies in their surgery unit. He was now considering moving closer to his family in Pennsylvania and would not mind joining the staff of the surgery unit at this hospital.

Later that year, the three brothers and their families reunited at John's house for Thanksgiving celebrations. The air was thick with nostalgia and the promise of shared memories. During the dinner, David's wife, Mary, and John's wife, Martha, reignited an old feud from their school days. The tension simmered beneath the surface, waiting for the right spark.

"Martha," Mary said sharply, her voice cutting through the noise. "It was you who told on me, wasn't it?" Her eyes locked onto Martha's, heavy with accusation.

Martha's cheeks reddened. "Mary, I—"

"Don't bother denying it," Mary interjected. "You went to the principal because you envied me."

The private school they attended had strict dress codes, and apparently, Mary had worn a skirt that violated this code. Martha's denial was swift, yet Mary insisted, claiming another friend had seen her speaking to the principal in her office.

"I was there discussing a Girl Scouts fundraiser, you fool," Martha retorted, her voice rising. "That's not true; you've always been jealous of me."

The room crackled with tension. But then, John—the peacemaker—stood up. His voice cut through the chaos, commanding attention. "Enough! Enough already." His gaze swept over the assembled family. "These petty squabbles about jealousy have divided us for many years. This is

Thanksgiving—a time to be appreciative of family, a time to recognize God's divine goodwill. Yet here we are, fighting over trivial matters."

He gestured toward the children, their eyes wide, absorbing every word. "We must set a positive example for them. Today, we have failed." His voice softened. "You two are going to drop this argument and reconcile now."

The room quieted down, the echoes of old wounds fading. And as they resumed their meal, the taste of forgiveness lingered—a bittersweet reminder that family was worth fighting for.

As the laughter echoed through the room, the three brothers and their families settled into a comfortable rhythm. The Thanksgiving feast unfolded as a collage of shared stories, clinking glasses, and the warmth of kinship.

Joshua's joke had broken the ice, and now it was David's turn. He leaned back in his chair, eyes twinkling. "Alright," he began, "I've got one for you all."

"Hit us with it!" John encouraged, wiping gravy from the corner of his mouth.

"So," David said, leaning in conspiratorially, "there was this elderly couple—married for decades. But their kids? Well, they were busy with their own lives, scattered across the country. The couple knew their children wouldn't visit for Thanksgiving."

The room leaned in, anticipation thickening the air. David continued, his voice dropping to a dramatic whisper. "The husband had a plan. He called each child, claiming he was divorcing their mother after forty years of marriage. Said he was going to marry a younger woman."

Gasps and chuckles erupted. Mary covered her mouth, eyes wide. "He didn't!"

"Oh, he did," David confirmed. "And he refused to listen to their pleas, hanging up the phone. But when the kids called their mother, she said, 'Well, I guess he's tired of seeing me after forty years.' And then she hung up on them."

The room erupted in laughter. Even the children, who'd initially thought the joke was lame, joined in. The absurdity of it—the lengths parents would go to bring their children home—struck a chord.

Later, in a cozy den on the other side of the house, Martha and Mary found themselves alone. The remnants of their earlier argument lingered, but now there was a softness in their eyes. Each apologized, their words tentative bridges across years of misunderstanding.

"I believe you," Mary said, her voice gentle. "About the snitching. Maybe it was June Bangor, the slender blonde. She always had a knack for stirring up trouble."

Martha nodded, tears glistening. "And I'm sorry too. Jealousy clouded my judgment."

They embraced, two women who'd carried old wounds. The room seemed to exhale, releasing decades of tension. Outside, the children played, their laughter a symphony of forgiveness.

David and his family had moved to Pennsylvania, joining the same hospital where their mother had been. The brothers, once fractured were now woven together. Their families gathered around the table, and as they held hands for grace, they knew that sometimes, healing came in the form of laughter, forgiveness, and the simple act of being together.

And so, in that moment, they gave thanks for the past, the present, and the promise of a future where love would bridge any divide.

8

"No Turning Back"

One Sunday, at church, a simple request to our organist, became a plea from the depths of my heart: "Play that song softly, please." His puzzled expression prompted the question, "Why do you want me to play it softly?" Words failed me, and all I could whisper was, "So as not to hurt those little kids again." The melody carried the weight of memories; memories of a time when the world was anything but soft.

To understand the silence behind my words, journey with me back to the 1990's, to Monrovia, Liberia, during their civil war. It was a decade when the city's heartbeat was gunfire, and its breath was the smoke of conflict. The residents, trapped in an unending nightmare, scrambled for safety amidst the chaos. Often taken between fires from warring factions, broken and demoralized they had to run for shelter. Foreign embassies became fortresses, trees and holes in the earth became sanctuaries, and the vast Atlantic Ocean became a desperate escape route for those who could brave its tides.

In this maelstrom, children lost their laughter as they were ripped from their parents' embrace by marauding troops. The innocence of youth was traded for the grim reality of war. Teenage boys, barely past childhood, were forced into the ranks of soldiers. A refusal meant death, and compliance meant the loss of their souls.

Amidst the violence, a church in the heart of the city stood as a beacon of hope, its walls promising protection. A congregation sought refuge within, praying for mercy from those who knew none. Their prayers went unanswered, their sanctuary desecrated, leaving behind only the echoes of their pleas and the shadows of their final moments. Piles of dead bodies, some terribly shattered were found in that church after the soldiers left, having fallen so thickly that some could not find room on the sanctuary's floor to die.

The war did not spare my own family. My father and uncle were taken by the cruelty of the conflict. Eyewitnesses recounted their brutal end, but closure remained elusive, their earthly traces lost to the ravages of war. In my heart, I seek solace in the belief that their souls have found peace beyond the reach of human strife.

In the aftermath of the civil war in Liberia, our congregation, a world away in the United States, felt a call to action. We adopted a school cradled in the slums skirting the edges of Monrovia. It became a beacon of hope, a testament to the resilience of the human spirit. We sent books to fill the shelves of their library, an electrical generator to illuminate their classrooms, and funds to expand several buildings and the sanctuary of learning they had come to cherish.

In March 2012, we journeyed to this war-scarred land to witness the fruits of our labor and to lay the foundation for a medical clinic. This clinic would stand as a symbol of healing, not just for the body but for the community's soul. As we traveled from the airport to the school, the landscape told a story of resilience. Despite the gaping wounds in buildings and the severed lifelines of electricity and water, there was an undeniable pulse of life, a rhythm of recovery.

Our hearts swelled with a mix of pride and humility as we saw the transformation our support had wrought. The school's library, once empty, now overflowed with knowledge. The buildings, once mere structures, now stood proudly completed. And the generator, a gift of light, promised continuity in the face of uncertainty.

Our journey brought us to the threshold of an orphanage, a sanctuary funded by a family within our congregation, their generosity rooted in the very soil of Liberia. This place stood as a bastion of hope for the war's youngest and most vulnerable survivors. Within its embrace, children blossomed amidst the remnants of turmoil, their spirits untarnished by the shadows of conflict that lingered in the air.

These young souls, boys with dreams as vast as the sky and girls with the poise of royalty, were clad in the armor of resilience. They were caretakers of life, shepherding cattle, and coaxing life from the earth in their gardens. More than anything, they were each other's keepers, their camaraderie a testament to the enduring human spirit. Their laughter and play, so akin to children thousands of miles away, belied the gravity of their past. It was a stark contrast to the nearby ruins, silent witnesses to humanity's folly where the quest for power had forsaken the ballot for the bullet.

During a Bible study, a profound exchange unfolded. The women of our group, seasoned in scripture, found themselves in awe of the children's profound grasp of the Bible's text and its deepest human teachings. As the day unfolded, it became clear that we were in the presence of young sages; their insights and understanding wove a new layer into the fabric of our faith, leaving us, the visitors, spellbound and humbled.

This encounter, rich with emotion and revelation, left an indelible mark on our hearts, forever changing our understanding of wisdom and the purity of faith witnessed in the eyes of children.

As I stood among these young souls, a question haunted me: "What kind of world allows its children to bear such burdens?" It is a question that lingers, a stain on the conscience of humanity. May we all seek forgiveness for the sins visited upon these innocents and strive to protect the purity that remains in our world.

In the heart of Africa, where life's trials are often most unforgiving, this orphanage is a cradle of hope amidst a landscape of adversity. Here, the love of God doesn't just visit; it resides, it thrives, it embraces each child with a warmth that defies the cold hand of rejection they've faced. The children, with their unyielding courage and boundless love, are beacons of hope in a world that has shown them its harshest face.

They carry no banners of self-pity, no flags of defeat. Instead, they stand united, a chorus of young hearts who have chosen a path of faith, following Jesus, their anchor in the storm. Their rendering of the song, "I have decided to follow Jesus," is not just a melody—it's their declaration, their testament to a strength that surpasses understanding. It resonates with a purity and conviction that could only come from souls that have seen darkness yet choose to walk in the light.

Imagine, if you will, the plight of being orphaned, cast aside, left to navigate the aftermath of war's cruel separation. Yet, in the midst of this, their voices rise, not in sorrow, but in joyous commitment, "The cross before me, the world behind me. No turning back, no turning back." It's a call that should echo through the hearts of all who hear it, believer or skeptic, for it carries the weight of genuine faith and the promise of hope.

As we prepared to leave the orphanage, the air was thick with emotion. Tears flowed freely, not just from the eyes of the children, but from the women among us, whose maternal instincts raged against the injustice these young ones endured. It was a poignant reminder of the deep-seated need to protect and nurture the innocent. Though we had to part, our support, our prayers, and our love would continue to reach across the oceans, a lifeline of solidarity for these remarkable children.

Their song, their spirit, and their unwavering resolve have left an indelible mark on my soul. In their voices, I heard not just a song, but a clarion call to all of humanity—to rise, to heal, to love.

As the sun sets on our journey, the echoes of the children's voices linger in the air, a haunting melody of resilience and hope. Their song, a beacon in the darkness of their past, guides them towards a future where love triumphs over loss. The orphanage stands as a testament to the strength of the human spirit, a place where the war's youngest victims find solace and the promise of a new day. In their unwavering gaze, we see the reflection of our own humanity, a reminder that amidst the deepest sorrows, there exists the potential for the greatest of joys. It is here, in the laughter and songs of these children, that we find the true essence of life's tapestry—woven not with threads of despair, but with strands of an unbreakable hope.

Before our visit, the hymn was a familiar melody, a Sunday routine. Now, it has transformed into an anthem of resilience, a testament to the enduring spirit that overcomes rejection. It's become a song of deep conviction, a reflection of the divine guidance that steers my life.

In the silent hours of the night, the children's voices haunt me, a poignant reminder of their enduring spirit that refuses to be silenced by the darkness of my sleepless nights. Their song, a soft murmur in my heart, is a plea for gentleness, a call to remember the fragility of innocence that war so carelessly shatters.

When the organ's notes begin to rise, I am transported back to those faces, to the echoes of their pain and the stark reality of war's indiscriminate cruelty. It's a pain that belongs to the purest among us, the children who look upon our world with eyes unclouded by malice. They, who see through the lens of simplicity and truth, do not deserve the harsh lessons taught by humanity's failures.

This is why I implore for softness in the music, for in its gentle strains lies the hope that we may one day learn to protect the peace and innocence that these children embody. Their song, now etched into the very essence of my being, is a constant reminder of what we must strive to preserve in this world.

Their pain and suffering inspired me to write this poem, not only for them but for children everywhere:

No Turning Back

A hostile world resolved to cease
    Kindness; on reckless wars embark,
Yet fair and bold lads sing of peace,
    "No turning back, no turning back."

Its weapons causing loss and pain
    With warring thugs in much delight,
Yet bright-eyed children in their strain
    Say, "peace;" dispel your sullied might.

Saved by conviction in their Lord
    Despite rejection, toil, and lack,
Yet, this they sing in one accord;
    "No turning back, no turning back."

In shadows deep, where silence speaks,
　　Of sorrows old and futures bleak,
Yet hopeful hearts, their comfort seek,
　　"No turning back, no turning back."

Through darkest nights and stormy days,
　　Their hearts steadfast, In spite of lack,
Their anthem strong, amidst the haze,
　　"No turning back, no turning back."

One with their savior and their Lord,
　　No fears from foul men's vile attack;
The cross, their light in troubled world,
　　"No turning back, no turning back."

In the quiet sanctuaries of our hearts, where hymns and scriptures reside, there often comes a moment, perhaps a divine whisper that breathes new life into words we've known by rote. It is a sacred awakening, unique to each soul, where no judgment casts its shadow, for every journey in faith is personal, every transformation, a testament to grace.

May this awakening stem not from the sorrows wrought by human hands, but from an innate yearning for spiritual depth and communal harmony. The tears of children caught in the crossfire of conflict should not be the catalyst for our understanding of divine teachings. War should never be the tutor of our conscience.

Let us instead be guided by the gentle hand of peace, for it is in the nurturing of tranquility that we shield the innocence of youth from the ravages of strife. In the pursuit of peace, let us forge a future where the laughter of children is a chorus that drowns out the clamor of discord, where their dreams are cradled in the promise of a world untainted by the specter of war.

9

Reunited

George Adams and his parents reside in Franklin Township, near Columbus, Ohio. George, a high school student, walks home with his friends each day after school. Along their route, they encounter three homeless men who often ask passersby for help in the form of money or food.

Most people barely notice these men, adrift like stray vessels in the vast sea. Some acknowledge them but quickly ignore them, rushing off as if preoccupied with world-saving tasks or medical breakthroughs. Yet, the dismissive behavior of some is disheartening—rolling their eyes or shouting at the men to find employment. In contrast, George and his friends make time to stop and chat with these individuals. While some of George's peers mock the men, their presence is welcomed. The students soon begin bringing food and money for the men, with George showing particular concern for their well-being. One afternoon, after returning home from school, George decides to go back and spend more time with them.

In the dimming light of the city, Edgar Norwich sits quietly in his wheelchair, the world around him a blur. The brown paper bag in his lap, a hushed testament to his daily battles, crinkles softly with each movement. George knows the stories that Edgar's eyes hold, the pain of a life that took a turn somewhere along the way.

George sees Edgar not as the "drunken, no-legs Edgar" that others whisper about, but as a man with a heart, a history, and a name. He approaches Edgar with respect, offering not just food, but a listening ear and a steady voice of encouragement. "You're more than this," George says, his words a gentle nudge towards hope.

Each sandwich George makes is more than sustenance; it's a symbol of care, a building block of trust. His parents, unknowing contributors to this nightly ritual, provide the means for these small acts of kindness. And though they attribute the extra food to their son's appetite, it's really George's compassion that's growing.

The sandwiches become a nightly expectation, a shared moment between George and the men, especially Edgar. With each bite, there's an unspoken promise from George—a promise to be there, to remember that everyone has a story worth hearing, and a life worth living.

Edgar's journey is a difficult one, but with George's support, there's a glimmer of possibility, a chance that the grip of alcohol might loosen. It's a slow process, filled with setbacks and triumphs, but George remains steadfast. For in Edgar, he sees not just a man in need, but a reflection of humanity's collective struggle and inherent worth.

One day, as George was walking home from school, he noticed Edgar sitting on a bench, looking unusually sober. His hair was neatly combed, his appearance fresh, and notably, the typical brown paper bag was absent from his hand. George took a seat next to Edgar, and they struck up a conversation. Initially hesitant, George eventually broached the subject of Edgar's missing lower limbs. Overcome with emotion, Edgar shared his story:

"I'm a veteran. My platoon and I were in a foxhole when the enemy lobbed two grenades at us. I threw myself on one to save my comrades. Fortunately, the second grenade didn't detonate, but the first one took my legs. My last memory before the coma was of being airlifted in a helicopter."

Edgar continued, his voice breaking, "After the war, my wife left me because of my injuries. I turned to alcohol to numb the pain and the nightmares. I thought no one cared, so I had nothing to live for. But talking to you... it gives me hope."

Moved by Edgar's candor, George felt grateful for resisting the urge to judge Edgar for his drunkenness. He handed Edgar some money from his allowance and walked home, reflecting on their exchange.

The following week, George returned with sandwiches, snacks, and drinks to learn more about Edgar's life. Edgar was again clean-shaven and sober, while the other men kept their distance. As they shared the food, Edgar reminisced about his comrades: Jimmy, the brave scout, who would scale the hills to spy on the enemy, returning to his platoon with enemy intelligence including their battlefield positioning and movements; Bobby, the fastidious teacher, who would rebuke them each time their language was incorrect or inappropriate, often stressing their positioning of subjects and objects in their spoken sentences; and Big Tommy, whose wife was expecting. Edgar's tales of camaraderie and survival in the face of fear left a profound impression on George. After their meal, George bid farewell and made his way home, carrying with him the weight and warmth of Edgar's stories.

In the evening, as the amber hues of sunset bled through the kitchen window, George's parents arrived home, their curiosity immediately piqued by the aroma of freshly made sandwiches. They questioned George about his recent voracious appetite, particularly his newfound hobby of crafting multiple sandwiches. With a gentle smile, George recounted his afternoons spent sharing meals with three homeless individuals, weaving in the poignant tale of Edgar Norwich, the man without a home but rich in stories.

Tom, George's father, absorbed his son's words, sinking into his chair as if the weight of a thousand memories pressed upon him. Silence enveloped the room, punctuated only by the soft ticking of the wall clock, until it was shattered by the sound of a single tear hitting the hardwood floor. Are you certain it was Edgar Norwich?" he whispered, his voice barely audible.

"Yes, Dad," George affirmed, his own eyes brimming with empathy. "But why the tears?"

Tom's gaze drifted to a faded photograph on the mantle, his mind traversing time and space back to the trenches of war, where camaraderie was forged in the crucible of conflict. "Edgar Norwich... he was my brother-in-arms, but I witnessed his fall in a forsaken foxhole. Could this man be weaving tales of deceit?"

George, steadfast in his conviction, shook his head. "He spoke of a comrade named Tommy, whose wife cradled hope for their unborn child amidst the chaos of war. He yearned for Tommy's safe return. We can visit him now, if you wish."

"That's him," Tom breathed, a torrent of realization washing over him. "But why, Dad? Why keep your valor in shadows? Your legacy is one to be heralded."

Tom clasped his son's hand, his eyes reflecting a mixture of pride and sorrow. "Thank you, my boy. War is a spectacle that often glorifies the few while the many suffer in silence like the men, women, and children, who are often innocent casualties of war. Each medal, each accolade, is but a mirror reflecting the cost of peace. As a soldier stares into the abyss, when dying on a battlefield with the enemy's tanks approaching, medals lose their luster, overshadowed by the pursuit of peace, as the good book implores. Your mother and I chose silence over soliloquies of war, for some memories are better left unspoken, lest they tarnish the beauty of the life we've built."

George nodded, a newfound maturity dawning within him. "I understand, Dad. Your silence is a testament to your strength. Thank you for your service, and for the love you've given me."

With a father's embrace, Tom whispered words of pride, sealing a moment of reconciliation and understanding between two generations touched by the echoes of war.

The evening's tender embrace held the town as George's mother, a silent witness of her family's concern, proposed a quest to find Edgar Norwich, the soul who had unwittingly knitted himself into the fabric of their lives. As they stepped into the world outside, the cosmos itself seemed to hold its breath, with only the stars and the moon's delicate curve as their lanterns in the night. Their car became a chariot of hope, cutting through the darkness to the corner that had become Edgar's unlikely throne. Yet, it lay deserted, an empty stage where the lead actor was missing. Despair began to whisper, but hope is a flame that darkness cannot smother. From the shadows, a figure emerged, his presence a silent testament to life's resilience. The moon graced his features, painting him in strokes of silver and shadow. Recognition sparked like a firework in Tom's heart. "That's him! That's him! He's alive! He's alive!" he cried, his voice a symphony of relief and joy. Tom's sprint was a race against all the fears of loss, his arms outstretched to enfold Edgar in an embrace that was both a greeting and a lifeline. It was an embrace that spoke of battles fought and won, of the fragile strength of the human spirit. One that almost broke whatever was left of Edgar's wheelchair. Together, they hugged, two souls anchored in a moment of pure, unspoken understanding, their tears an ocean of shared humanity.

Tom invited Edgar to spend the night at his house, so the family helped Edgar into their car. As the car pulled away from the reunion, the journey home was a bridge between past and present. Edgar, surrounded by Tom's family, felt a sense of belonging that had eluded him for years. The conversation flowed easily, a mix of laughter and poignant silence as landmarks sparked memories of youth and dreams unburdened by war.

That night, under Tom's roof, the walls listened to stories of valor and camaraderie. Tom expressed his gratitude to Edgar, not just for saving his life, but for being the brother he chose in the trenches of uncertainty. Edgar, humble as ever, redirected the praise to George, whose selfless act was the cornerstone of their survival.

The revelation of George's conception during the war added a layer of serendipity to the narrative. It was as if fate had woven their lives together long before they knew it. Edgar's bravery ensured that Tom would live to see the birth of his son, George. Tom's support in helping Edgar find employment and a place to call home was more than an act of charity; it was an affirmation of their unbreakable bond.

Edgar's new beginning was marked not by the absence of his legs, but by the abundance of his spirit. No longer adrift, he had found his anchor in the family he formed with those who stood by him when the world was a battlefield. In the quiet of the night, as Tom and Edgar shared memories, they didn't just recount history—they forged a future where hope was the victor and friendship was the spoils of their war.

Three months later, Edgar was fitted with prosthetic legs. The reunion of the men was an assortment of feelings pieced together with strands of nostalgia, joy, and an unspoken understanding of the sacrifices made. Edgar, standing tall on his new prosthetic legs, felt a surge of pride and gratitude. With him were the friends who had been with him in that foxhole when he lost his legs: Tom, George's dad; Jim Jones (Jimmy), the brave one; Robert Johnson (Bobby), the school teacher; Brad Forsythe, a guitarist; and Lamar Cole, an attorney. They were all grateful for his bravery and sacrifice. As Edgar looked into the eyes of his comrades—Tom, whose paternal strength had been a pillar of support; Jim, whose courage had never wavered; Robert, whose wisdom had often been their saving grace; Brad, whose melodies had lifted their spirits; and Lamar, whose legal acumen had been a shield—they all shared a moment of silent acknowledgment. Their bond, forged in the crucible of war, was unbreakable.

They raised their glasses, not just to Edgar's bravery, but to the enduring spirit of friendship and to the love that had blossomed in the aftermath of adversity. It was a celebration of life, a testament to the resilience of the human spirit, and a tribute to the young man, George Adams, whose legacy lived on in the joyful eyes of a little boy named in his honor.

Later, the hospital corridors that once echoed with the uncertainty of recovery now resonated with the laughter of Edgar's children, little George, who was named after George Adams, and Suzie, chasing each other, their giggles a sweet symphony to his ears.

His wife, the compassionate nurse who had once tended to his wounds, now stood by his side, her hand a reassuring weight on his shoulder. Their love, a beacon that guided him through the darkest times, now illuminated their lives with warmth and tenderness.

Often, the group of men would get together in the summer to celebrate their lives, and their families have become quite close. One summer, they met in Virginia Beach, and Brad, the guitarist, composed a song which he played, and they all sang with gusto:

Serenade Of Peace

Endless peace, not as the world gives,
  From senseless pain and blight release;
In hearts of valiant men it lives,
  This fragile world, its wars may cease.

Endless peace for you and for me;
  Uncle, aunty, nephew and niece,
Father, mother, daughter can be
  The dear lover of endless peace.

Endless peace, like the flowing seas,
  Availed for minds to be at ease.
One is remiss if the eyes sees
  Not the virtue of endless peace.

In silent whispers, calls to all,
  A gentle plea in night's soft fall.
May each soul heed its tender call,
  And lift us all, before we fall.

For in the end, what matters most;
  The peace we've found, the love we host.
In every heart, it'll be the boast,
  Man's endless peace, our cherished toast.

So let us join in quest so bright,
  For endless peace, for endless light.
Then hand in hand, with all our might,
  We'll efface sadness and its blight.

10

Son of a Father

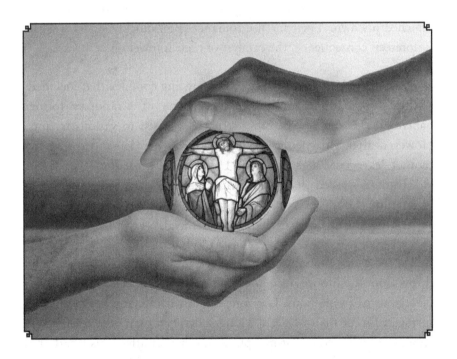

My name is Bill, and I am the progeny of a man named George. To the world, he is my father, but the term feels foreign on my tongue. I cannot conjure memories of paternal warmth or guidance from him. Our shared features and DNA are mere echoes of a lineage, not the bonds of fatherhood. George's entry into this world came late in his own father's life. My grandfather, a man of success and ambition, lavished his affection and resources on George, his sole heir born of his old age. Owning a string of haberdasheries and a portfolio of real estate in Manchester, Maryland, Grandpa ensured George's future was secure, placing his wealth in trust for his young son.

By the time my existence began to unfold, George had already let half of that fortune slip through his fingers. His life was a spectacle of excess—speeding cars, ephemeral loves, and wild soirees. Yet, amidst this decadence, he clung to a semblance of responsibility, running a private business with intermittent dedication. It was in this whirlwind of life that he encountered my mother, Jody, a woman whose passion for life matched his own. Their intense romance spun quickly, and I was the unforeseen consequence, the catalyst of their unraveling.

We briefly lived on George's estate, a sprawling complex that included: a three-story, single family residence, one of Grandpa's former haberdasheries and several other structures leased to various tenants. However, after a particularly wild night, George demanded that my mother leave with her children. I was a mere toddler—two years old. Rumors swirled that a bar-owning mistress had given George an ultimatum: choose her or lose her. My mother, once envisioning George as her knight, was left shattered by his betrayal.

Exiled from the estate, we found refuge in a humble abode, a stone's throw from the life we once knew. There, my mother's heartache over George turned venomous. I became the unwitting target of her rage, a surrogate for the man who had wronged her. Her fury, once reserved for George, now lashed out at me, punishing me for affections I harbored for the man she despised. In her eyes, I was the architect of their failed love story, and her resentment spilled over in harsh words and harsher hands. Any tenderness I showed George was met with her wrath, a bitter reminder of the love lost, and the dreams dashed.

George's presence in my life was like a distant star—visible, yet cold and remote. Our weekend encounters were sporadic, and during those brief interludes, his world seemed to orbit around everything but me. He adorned me in lavish attire, not out of affection, but as a barbed message to my mother, a display of his financial prowess. Memories of him helping with homework or sharing in fatherly activities are absent from my childhood narrative.

The injustice my mother endured ignited a fire within her, propelling her to seek legal avenues for support. She pursued child support, a beacon of hope for a more stable future for us. However, George's response to the court's mandate was one of defiance; he withheld the support, dragging us back into the legal fray. I was an unwitting participant in their courtroom drama, my presence a silent testimony to the dispute over my upbringing.

During one pivotal hearing, the magistrate, moved by my mother's plight, dangled the threat of incarceration over George for his noncompliance. The outcome was a compromise: I would stay with my mother, while George was allotted visitation rights. In the shadow of the courthouse, my mother's words became my script, her fears instilled in me the gravity of each word I would speak. Her manipulation was a strategy born of desperation, and I, a child caught in the crossfire, complied.

The pendulum of my life swung between two homes—my mother's abode and George's domain. Every other weekend, George would retrieve me, introducing me to a revolving door of partners. Their attitudes towards me varied like the seasons—some were warm and nurturing, others cold and indifferent. It was from these encounters that I gleaned lessons of kindness and compassion, traits that I vowed to embody. A partner of my mother's would often take me to ball games, clothe me, and tend to my needs, while a woman in my father's life ensured I never went hungry. These gestures, small yet profound, imprinted upon me the value of generosity. Conversely, the harshness of others taught me resilience and the importance of empathy. Each person, whether they realized it or not, contributed a thread to the fabric of my being, shaping the person I am today.

The abrupt halt of child support payments from George was like a winter chill that swept through our home, leaving us without the warmth of basic necessities. School supplies became luxuries, and even food became scarce. My mother, driven to the edge of desperation, turned to the authorities. Her actions were not just a cry for help but a battle cry against the man who had let us down. When the law finally caught up with George, my mother's reaction was a mix of vindication and relief, her words echoing through our home like a victory chant.

George's stint in jail was brief, thanks to my uncle's intervention, but his subsequent flight to Brazil felt like an abandonment all over again. At the tender age of six, the concept of "father" became synonymous with absence and silence. The void he left was as profound as the ocean between us.

As time marched on, the echoes of my parents' discordant relationship weighed on me, a constant reminder of a bond broken. Yet, in the midst of this emotional maelstrom, I found solace in compliance and education. Adhering to my mother's expectations became my shield, a way to deflect her frustrations. My focus on academics was less about the pursuit of knowledge and more about seeking her approval, a temporary balm for her tempestuous spirit. This strategy became my lifeline, a way to navigate the turbulent waters of our lives. Even as rumors of George's fleeting presence fluttered around me, their truth as elusive as the man himself, I clung to my books and the promise they held for a different future.

At fifteen, life handed me a letter from George, delivered by my uncle's hands. It was an attempt at penance, a written apology for the years of absence. But the words fell flat, like autumn leaves long after the season had passed. Each sentence was a reminder of the void he had left, a space where echoes of missed milestones and absent affections resided. His remorse, now confined to ink and paper, could not stir the numbness that had settled in my heart. The letter was a relic of a relationship that never was, a specter of a father who existed in name but not in deed.

The indifference that met his words was not born of spite but of survival. The emotional chasm his abandonment had created was bridged by my own resilience, not by his belated regrets. His absence had taught me self-reliance, to find solace in solitude, and to draw strength from the void where paternal love never took root.

The years of neglect and the responsibility of carrying the fallout from a failed adult relationship hastened my maturity. For better or worse, these experiences have indelibly shaped my upbringing and my understanding of resilience.

At seventeen, I began my college journey, filled with a zeal for learning. My mother lived in a quaint house in Hampstead, Maryland. One brisk December afternoon during winter recess, I returned from college. The air was crisp, and the sky, a muted grey, seemed to grieve in silence. Bare branches stood as stoic guardians, their foliage long shed, now a crunchy spectacle of brown and gold underfoot. The sun, a dimmed beacon veiled in mist, provided scant warmth, its weak rays barely cutting through the cloud cover. A piercing wind meandered through the streets, its breath laced with the aroma of woodsmoke and the hint of impending snow. It was the sort of afternoon that rendered one's breath visible, a spectral mist in the frigid air, stirring a longing for the solace of a warm fireplace. Amidst this wintry backdrop, her words struck with the sharpness of falling icicles, breaking the delicate quiet. "Did you hear your father passed away?" my mother said, her tone nonchalant, almost cheerful. That was how I learned of George's demise. Her apathy seemed as frosty as the air around us; it appeared that forgiveness was an alien concept to her heart.

In the solitude of my room, I became a silent historian, piecing together the fragments of a past that might have been. The scarcity of joyful memories with George was a stark canvas, void of the vibrant hues of fatherly love. No images of him cheering from the sidelines, no recordings of birthday candles extinguished by wishes he never heard. Yet, in the quiet moments, I sought to resurrect the faint echoes of his existence, offering a prayer into the void he left behind.

The concept of abandonment, especially of one's own flesh and blood, is a riddle wrapped in the enigma of human nature. The animal kingdom shows us that even the most ferocious beasts nurture their young. But George, in his abandonment, defied this primal duty, casting a pall of hardship and loneliness over an innocent life. His departure sentenced me to navigate a world where familial ties are the norm, and yet I was adrift, an invisible entity weighed down by his absence.

In the wake of such desertion, my abandoned soul wandered, a specter in a world teeming with familial bonds. I was the unseen, moving through life with the weight of absence heavy on my shoulders. The void left by George's departure was a void too vast to bridge, a silent scream in the cacophony of my life's orchestra. Forsaken like a tender sapling uprooted, I had to weather the storm of life unshielded. Bereft of fatherly guidance, my path was strewn with thorns of doubt and stones of sorrow. Trust became a treasure lost to the abyss of betrayal, and love became a concept as alien as the stars that watch indifferently from above.

Scrutinizing George's actions, one might wonder if fear, perhaps of my mother's wrath or the repercussions of his own misdeeds, steered his course. Did the unearned inheritance from his father embolden his neglect? Or did his intoxicated delusions elevate him to a god-like status, decreeing my suffering as some divine test? Unlike the messianic sacrifices of lore, my trials bore no sanctity, no grand design. I was but a child, a life he ushered into being, deserving of the most basic offerings of care and affection.

George, far removed from any semblance of divinity, spared the world the misfortune of his rule. His selfishness, a trait all too human, rendered him unworthy of the title "father" and undeserving of the love of a son such as myself.

Yet, within the narrative of my life, hatred finds no sanctuary. My heart, seasoned by trials, has learned the grace of forgiveness. It is not a weakness but a strength that has emerged from the depths of poverty, neglect, and scorn. I stand not with bitterness, but with a spirit of gratitude for the resilience that has been my companion and the deliverance that has been my salvation. Forgiveness, the ever-present guardian, has taught me that even in the absence of a father's love, one can find the means to love oneself and forge a path forward.

I wrote this poem to encapsulate my experience with George:

What Is There To Love?

What is there to love about a man,
    Who'd litter earth, caring not his deed,
Who'd ne'er face a mere guileless lad's span,
    Surrendering sway to mold and build?

I'd like to love him much as I could,
    But barely saw him, to feel his warmth.
Should I just imagine that he would
    Be a doting dad, despite his dearth?

Perhaps, feared he'd be inadequate,
    On toddler trips, things of puberty.
Give him his due, one must ne'er equate,
    Courage and cowardice in duty.

Did he hear the cries from his lad's voice?
    Did he feel the yearning for dad's love?
Yet his shameless mind made the sad choice,
    Being a reckless soul, and ties dissolve.

Perhaps, I should hate him for disdain,
    Perhaps, seek requite for these effects;
Desertion, depression, and their pain,
    Yet, inclined to forgive and forget.

He had it all, resources, and brain,
    Enough to mold and sustain his clone.
What is there to love about a man,
    Who has it all, yet desert his own?

The revelation of George's flight from the country unveiled a panorama of misdeeds and desperation. His evasion of child support was but the tip of an iceberg, beneath which lay a labyrinth of dubious dealings and financial irresponsibility. The specter of legal retribution and the IRS's looming shadow spurred him to liquidate his assets, leaving behind a trail of unsettled debts and broken promises.

In Brazil, George's path crossed with Carmelita, whose beauty was matched only by her dangerous liaisons. Seduced by her allure and the promise of lucrative investments, he found himself ensnared in a web of deceit. The real estate venture, a mirage crafted by the hands of a cartel, evaporated along with his funds. His attempt to seek justice backfired, igniting the wrath of those he sought to expose. The tragic outcome was a grim dance with fate that claimed not only his life but also that of his unsuspecting brother, who was visiting.

The assailants, shadows wielding the power of life and death, carried out their orders with chilling efficiency. The Brazilian authorities' efforts to untangle the truth were thwarted by a lack of evidence, leaving the story of George and his brother shrouded in the mists of uncertainty.

George's demise is a cautionary tale, a stark illustration of the consequences that can befall those who stray from the path of integrity. His life, a patchwork of choices, serves as a lesson in the perils of succumbing to the darker impulses of human nature. In contrast, I have chosen to forge a different legacy—one built on the pillars of generosity, fidelity, and responsibility. As a parent, I am committed to nurturing these virtues, to be the beacon of guidance that George never was. This is the inheritance I claim—not one of wealth or material gain, but of character and moral fortitude. It is the legacy I will pass on, the true wealth of a father's love; the legacy I choose to embrace as the son of a father.

11

The Hopeless Kid

Mrs. Denton, with her stern gaze magnified behind thick spectacles, was the epitome of discipline within the hallowed halls of Delaware's high school education. Her reputation for unwavering strictness was as well-known as it was formidable, leaving little room for leniency in her meticulously structured classroom. Students who dared to deviate from her precise teaching methods or faltered in following her exacting instructions felt the full weight of her disapproval.

In the year of 1990, young Dennis Gallo found himself navigating the choppy waters of adolescence while seated in Mrs. Denton's class, a place where order reigned supreme. Outside the classroom walls, his world was unraveling; the canvas of his family life torn asunder by his parents' bitter separation. The tremors of their domestic upheaval reverberated through every aspect of his life, leaving his schoolwork as tattered as his sense of stability. Assignments, once completed with care, were now handed in late—if they managed to be submitted at all—caught in the crossfire of legal skirmishes, the heartache of a home sold, and the raw wounds of a custody battle.

Mrs. Denton, ever the bastion of rigor, could not see the silent battle behind Dennis' weary eyes, nor the turmoil that churned beneath his stoic facade. It was a time of emotional tempests for Dennis, a season of life where the sanctuary of education became yet another battlefield, and the compassion he so desperately needed was obscured by the shadow of expectation.

Unsympathetic to Dennis' plight, Mrs. Denton deemed him "hopeless." One day, she marched into the principal's office, Dennis reluctantly in tow, and insisted he be placed in a class for "slower" students. "Dennis is a slow learner," she asserted, "and will benefit from a more paced learning environment." The principal, trusting Mrs. Denton's judgment, bypassed further inquiry and acquiesced to her recommendation. Dennis' parents, consumed by their own troubles, concurred with the school's decision, and thus, Dennis was relegated to the so-called "slower" class.

It was there that Dennis met Mr. Davis, a teacher who quickly recognized Dennis' latent talents. Contrary to Mrs. Denton's assessment, Dennis was not only capable but also excelled, often assisting his peers academically. Mr. Davis, curious about Dennis' transfer, uncovered the impact of his parents' separation on his academic performance, yet it was evident that Dennis' intellect remained intact. Grateful for Dennis' contributions, Mr. Davis utilized his skills to facilitate group learning, with Dennis often leading his classmates in exercises involving math, English writing, and comprehension.

Dennis' academic journey did not end there. He graduated from high school, pursued higher education, and aspired to practice law. Throughout college, Mr. Davis maintained contact, offering guidance and support. Over time, a strong bond formed between them, rooted in mutual respect and friendship.

While attending law school, Dennis encountered Jane Denton, who, unbeknownst to him, was the daughter of his former high school teacher, Mrs. Denton. Dennis was immersed in corporate law, while Jane was dedicated to criminal law. Their paths converged, and love blossomed after their graduation as they embarked on successful careers at the same law firm in upstate New York. As their relationship flourished, they envisioned a future together: marriage, children, and establishing their own law practice.

Their weekends unfurled like the pages of a storybook, each moment at the lakefront a serene brushstroke on the canvas of their memories. The sun's golden rays danced upon the water's surface, a glittering ballet that beckoned them to the water's edge. They would spend hours there, lost in the simple joy of each other's company, their laughter mingling with the gentle lapping of the waves.

Local eateries became their culinary sanctuary, where the flavors of the region were served with a side of warm hospitality. Each meal was an adventure, a chance to explore the myriad of tastes that the local chefs wove with pride and passion.

As the seasons turned, the lake effect snow draped the landscape in a pristine white cloak, transforming the familiar into a wonderland of sparkling frost. They embraced the chill, finding warmth in shared hot cocoa and the soft crunch of snow beneath their boots as they explored the frosted forests.

Nearby ski resorts offered a rush of adrenaline to contrast the peacefulness of the lake, their slopes a playground for the daring. Together, they carved paths through the snow, their hearts racing with the thrill of the descent.

In the evenings, they retreated to the cozy embrace of a lakeside cabin, where the crackling fire was a symphony to accompany their intertwined conversations. There, wrapped in blankets and the comfort of each other's presence, they spoke of dreams and whispered secrets, the bond between them a silent promise, as enduring as the stars that watched over them.

The time had come to introduce their families. Dennis and Jane first visited Dennis' parents, who, despite their divorce, shared a harmonious relationship from their separate homes in New Jersey. The encounter was warm and welcoming; Dennis' father, a civil engineer with a penchant for detail, joined them at his ex-wife's residence. Both parents were instantly charmed by Jane, admiring her poise, authenticity, and warmth.

During a heartfelt conversation, Jane expressed her admiration for Dennis, praising his exceptional qualities and the love he had shown her. She gratefully acknowledged his parents for nurturing such a remarkable man. The evening culminated in a delightful dinner featuring halibut, mashed potatoes, and a selection of Californian white wine. In a moment of celebration, Dennis announced their engagement, eliciting exuberant cheers from his elated parents.

Next, it was time to meet the Dentons. Upon arriving at their home, Dennis was struck by a realization: Jane's mother, the retired teacher who had once deemed him "hopeless," was none other than Mrs. Denton. Despite this, Dennis approached the situation with grace. He expressed gratitude to Mrs. Denton for transferring him to the class for "slower" students, explaining that it was inadvertently what he needed at the time. "What do you mean it was just what you needed?" Mrs. Denton inquired, puzzled. Dennis elaborated on his parents' separation and the lack of support he faced with his schoolwork as they grappled with their own issues.

Mrs. Denton, taken aback, questioned why Dennis had never confided in her. He candidly responded, "To be honest, Mrs. Denton, your strictness was intimidating, and I wasn't alone in my fear. Furthermore, you never inquired about the reasons behind my incomplete homework." The tension in the room grew palpable until Mr. Denton, seeking to lighten the mood, offered to show Dennis his new golf clubs. "That would be nice, sir. What brand are they?" Dennis asked, eager to divert the conversation. "I'm not certain, but it starts with a 'T'," Mr. Denton replied.

As the two men stepped away, Jane confronted her mother, dismayed by her past actions. Mrs. Denton, filled with regret, admitted her mistake and expressed her sorrow for not being more approachable to her students. When Dennis and Mr. Denton returned, Mrs. Denton apologized directly to Dennis, who graciously accepted her words. He then joyfully shared his plans to marry Jane, to which the Dentons responded with elation and blessings.

The summer wedding of Dennis and Jane was nothing short of enchanting, set against the serene backdrop of a quaint church in upstate New York. The church's historic walls, adorned with vibrant stained glass, echoed with melodies of love as the couple exchanged their heartfelt vows.

As the afternoon sun cast a golden glow, the celebration transitioned to a grand lakefront reception. The air was filled with the sweet scent of blooming flowers, and the gentle lapping of the lake's waters against the shore provided a tranquil soundtrack. Nearly two hundred guests mingled on the lush green lawns, their laughter and joy contributing to the festive atmosphere.

Among the esteemed guests was Mr. Davis, a figure of inspiration in Dennis' life. Having taught Dennis in a class designed for students needing a gentler pace of learning, Mr. Davis's presence was a testament to the profound impact he had on Dennis' journey. Now retired, Mr. Davis attended the joyous occasion with his wife, sharing in the celebration of a student he had seen grow and flourish.

The reception was a feast for the senses, with tables laden with delectable cuisine and the air resonant with the clinking of glasses in toasts to the newlyweds.

During the festivities, the groomsman delivered a heartfelt poem to the newlyweds. It reads:

Writ in Fate: A Love's Ode

Doting hearts entwined, bound as one
    In love, endure the test of time,
No more are you each one alone,
    But will concur in time and rhyme.

Your budding love so far has shown,
    There's joy and bliss writ in your fate,
Though you may trek through the unknown
    True love like yours surely does great.

As seasons change and years will pass,
    Through trials faced and vict'ries won,
Your union, strong, will surely last;
    As one, shine like the morning sun.

May you be blessed with living flow'rs
    Like lovely kids, that heav'n endow'rs;
Your joys win out in coming years
    And laughter drowns those stubborn tears.

So here's to you, the bride and groom,
    May your days be full of laughter loud,
To Dennis and Jane, one in name,
    In the dance of life, ever proud.

As the evening sky transitioned to a canvas of stars, the dance floor came alive with the rhythmic beats of music, inviting everyone to partake in the revelry.

It was a day where every moment was savored, memories were made, and the union of Dennis and Jane was celebrated with an outpouring of love and happiness that would be cherished for years to come.

Indeed, the irony was palpable: a boy once dismissed as hopeless by a teacher now stood as the husband of that teacher's daughter. At the reception's conclusion, Justin, a friend of Dennis and a medical doctor, approached Mrs. Denton. Recognition flickered in her eyes, yet she couldn't place him. Justin gently reminded her that he, too, had been in her class and was recommended for transfer to the "slower" students' class. It was Dennis who had mentored him there, and their bond had remained strong over the years. He expressed gratitude for her service before departing.

This encounter left Mrs. Denton visibly shaken; she retreated to the ladies' room, overwhelmed by emotion and stayed there until her husband's call for them to leave. Later, at home, she confided in her husband about the distressing realization of her misjudgments—not only regarding Dennis but Justin as well—and feared how many others she might have failed. The weight of this revelation took a toll on her.

As the tropical sun dipped below the horizon, painting the Hawaiian sky with strokes of orange and pink, Dennis and Jane's laughter echoed through the balmy air, their hearts light with the bliss of newlywed euphoria. They strolled hand in hand along the sandy shores, oblivious to the world beyond their cocoon of happiness.

Meanwhile, miles away, the Denton household was enveloped in a somber shadow that contrasted starkly with the bright cheer of the island paradise. Mrs. Denton, a woman once vibrant as the garden she tenderly nurtured, now found herself in the throes of an invisible storm.

Depression, like a relentless downpour, drenched her days in shades of gray, the colors of her life leaching away with each passing moment.

The medication prescribed to her was meant to be a lifeline, a beacon to guide her back to herself. Yet, in a moment of despair so profound it swallowed her whole, that very lifeline seemed to become a chain that pulled her deeper into the abyss. The afternoon Mr. Denton found her, the kitchen—a place once filled with the aroma of baked delights and the warmth of shared stories—had transformed into a silent witness to her pain.

The ride to the hospital was a blur of sirens and flashing lights, a stark contrast to the serene quiet of the golf course that Mr. Denton had left behind. He sat by her bedside, his hand gripping hers, a silent plea for her return. The beeping of the machines punctuated the stillness, a reminder of the fragility of life.

Mr. Denton's heart was torn. Part of him yearned to reach out to Dennis and Jane, to share the burden that weighed so heavily on his shoulders. Yet, he couldn't bear to cast a cloud over their sunshine, to pull them back from their idyllic escape into the storm that raged at home. So, he chose to shoulder the silence, a solitary sentinel keeping watch over the woman who had been his partner in life's dance.

In the quiet of the hospital room, as he watched over his wife, Mr. Denton's thoughts drifted to the memories they shared—their joys, their sorrows, and the unspoken promises of "in sickness and in health." It was a test of love and endurance, a moment that distilled the essence of their vows into the silent language of presence and hope.

And so, as the night deepened, Mr. Denton remained, a beacon of steadfast love, while across the ocean, Dennis and Jane continued to dance under the stars, their hearts light, their future unwritten, and their past momentarily out of sight.

The air was thick with tension as Dennis and Jane, fresh from the bliss of their Hawaiian retreat, stepped into the sterile hospital corridors. The scent of antiseptics and the hushed tones of the staff were a stark contrast to the vibrant, carefree laughter that had surrounded them just days before. They found Mrs. Denton, a pillar in their lives, now a portrait of resilience, her eyes reflecting a journey through the darkest valleys of the soul.

Her week in the hospital had been a crucible, burning away the chaff of past perceptions and leaving behind the kernel of hard-earned wisdom. As she sat across from Dr. Evelyn Pringle, whose reputation for unraveling the tangled threads of the psyche preceded her, Mrs. Denton felt the weight of years of unexamined judgments lift from her shoulders. Dr. Pringle's office, a sanctuary of understanding, became the ground where Mrs. Denton planted the seeds of her rebirth.

Dr. Pringle's words, like a gentle but persistent rain, watered those seeds. "It is often shameful how the world judges and condemns others based on perceived deficiencies or differences. Who are we to deem someone hopeless or unworthy? Many who were once overlooked have ascended to remarkable heights." These words struck a chord, echoing in the hollows of Mrs. Denton's heart, filling them with a harmony that had long been silent.

With each session, Mrs. Denton peeled back the layers of her own preconceptions, revealing a tender core of empathy that had been shielded from the world's harshness. She began to see that students are not vessels to be filled, but individual universes, each with their own orbits of challenges and triumphs. She now understands that the classroom is a garden where young minds could bloom, nurtured by patience and understanding.

Emboldened by her own healing, Mrs. Denton became a beacon of hope to her colleagues in education. She shared her story with an open heart, her voice a soft but firm call to action. She spoke of the invisible struggles that many carry, the silent pleas for help that often go unheard, and the profound impact a moment of compassion can have on a young life.

Her advocacy rippled through the halls of education, inspiring a shift towards a more empathetic approach to teaching. Mrs. Denton's journey through the depths of despair and back into the light was a testament to the human spirit's capacity for change and the transformative power of empathy. In the twilight of her career, she had become not just a teacher of subjects, but a teacher of hearts, her legacy one of love and understanding that would echo through the generations.

12

The Mirror

From the tender years of middle school, my world revolved around the pursuit of beauty—a relentless quest that consumed my waking hours. My parents, lost in the demands of their work, entrusted my care to a Brazilian au pair. She was a kind spirit, her presence in our home as gentle as a whisper, ensuring my basic needs were met while she immersed herself in her studies. Her nonintrusive nature granted me the freedom to explore the realms of beauty that beckoned me with open arms.

The television was my gateway to a world where glamour reigned supreme, each beauty commercial a window into a life I yearned to claim as my own. I would sit, eyes glued to the screen, eagerly awaiting the next parade of flawless models and the promise of perfection they offered. When the screen offered no solace, I turned to my mother's sanctuary—the bathroom. There, amidst the array of beauty products, I found my playground.

The mirror became my stage, and I, the star performer. With each stroke of lipstick, each dusting of powder, I transformed into the embodiment of the elegance I admired. The reflection that stared back at me was not just a child playing dress-up; it was the emergence of a self-assured beauty, one who could rival the icons that flickered on the screen.

In those moments, alone with the mirror, I discovered a confidence that was both exhilarating and daunting. The belief that I was more beautiful, that I wore makeup with a grace that surpassed the professionals, was a secret thrill that danced in my heart. It was a silent rebellion against the images that defined beauty for the masses, a declaration that I, too, could claim a spot among the pantheon of the beautiful.

This emotional odyssey through the looking glass was more than a child's imitation of adulthood; it was the awakening of an identity, the shaping of a self-image that would carry me through the years. It was the beginning of a lifelong dance with beauty, a dance that promised both joy and heartache in its complex choreography.

High school was a time of transformation, where the allure of beauty became my compass, guiding me through the labyrinth of adolescence. The girls I surrounded myself with were like stars in a constellation, each one shining with their own unique brilliance. I found myself orbiting them, drawn in by their radiance, hoping to absorb just a fraction of their glow. The makeup brands—Revlon, L'Oréal, Avon, COVERGIRL—were my tools of metamorphosis, each product a brushstroke in the masterpiece I was attempting to create of myself.

The beauty pageants were my arena, a place where I could showcase the fruits of my labor. Each competition was a chance to validate my efforts, to prove that I too could shine as brightly as the girls I admired. The losses, though few, stung with the sharpness of betrayal, but I dismissed them as nothing more than the result of prejudiced eyes unable to recognize true beauty.

My mother, a bastion of traditional values, stood like a lighthouse amidst the tumultuous sea of modern beauty standards. Her perplexity at my obsession with appearance was as deep as the roots of an ancient oak. She held firm to the belief that character and kindness were the true measures of a person, not the fleeting judgments of superficial eyes. The pressure to conform and avoid the sting of ridicule at school was an alien concept to her, one that clashed with her time-honored principles.

In stark contrast, my father, a quite successful real estate investor, loves me very much, yet spent little time with me. I often joked that his real estate business was his first love because for most of the day, he would be out making deals, buying and selling properties. He navigated the world with a laissez-faire attitude, his actions seemingly detached yet subtly supportive. He would open his wallet to fund my quests for aesthetic perfection, perhaps seeing them as harmless diversions that kept me from disturbing the waters of his business focus. His reassurances to my mother were gentle but dismissive, "Lorie will outgrow this phase with time," he'd say, his voice a soothing balm to her worries.

College life, with its myriad social interactions, proved challenging; juggling late-night study sessions, assignment completions, looming deadlines, and attending classes—some of which seemed irrelevant to my nursing major. For instance, the necessity for a nursing student to take a political science course baffles me. It strikes me as a ploy by the establishment to extract money from students.

However, it was the presence of a dormmate named Sarah that made life particularly taxing. She appeared to have it all: a middle-class upbringing with professional parents, a humble demeanor, and a subtle, enchanting beauty—seemingly oblivious to her own charm. Her luscious hair cascaded down her back, stopping just above her slender waist. Her eyes sparkled with an ethereal glow, and her flawless skin seemed to never require lotion, radiating a natural luminescence. These traits were complemented by her impeccable legs, unmarred cheeks, and captivating allure.

Sarah exuded a natural affluence yet remained down-to-earth and approachable. She was always ready to lend a hand with homework, share her modest means, including money and food. If a friend was in trouble, she was the first to offer support. Essentially, she was the heart of the dorm, attracting everyone with her magnetic personality. She had a knack for making her friends smile during tense moments, lightening the atmosphere. Her encouragement for contentment with life's simplicities was infectious. Being in her presence felt like being touched by a benevolent spirit, regardless of the occasion.

Many boys were drawn to Sarah, the undisputed gem of our college. I once caught wind of a rumor that a boy had skipped classes just to bask in her presence—an act I found utterly absurd. Sarah's hallmark was her modesty; she treated everyone equally, regardless of their status. It was this trait, I believe, that made her truly captivating. Yet, the boys would gaze at her, scrutinizing her features with an almost surgical precision. I'm convinced that if they devoted as much effort to their studies, they'd effortlessly excel in every course and exam.

I must confess, my envy of Sarah ran deep. I yearned to emulate her, or even surpass her allure. When Sarah wasn't around, boys would engage me in conversation, but in her presence, I stood no chance. They ogled her like famished lions, and the girls clamored for her friendship—all except me. My feelings toward Sarah bordered on loathing, akin to the animosity between a lion and a pesky hyena. Despite my desire to mirror her beauty and dynamic presence, I had no interest in her companionship. I aspired to be the center of attention.

Thus, the mirror became my confidant, and beauty salons, my sanctuaries. Within months, I transformed from what I considered a pretty girl to a stunning beauty—or so I believed. I garnered more friends, more admiring glances, and a flurry of lunch and dinner invitations from young men. This newfound popularity buoyed my spirits, yet it paled in comparison to Sarah's enduring circle of devoted friends. Each week, I'd gain a few acquaintances but lose others for myriad reasons. The more friends I lost, the more I experimented with various beauty products and frequented different salons.

Eventually, I opted for a larger, ornate mirror to better scrutinize my features, as my old one seemed too diminutive and dated. My gaze would critically wander over my body, cataloging every detail in my mind. However, the more I observed, the more dissatisfaction crept in, leading me to consider plastic surgery. For this, I turned to my affluent parents, particularly my father, who was ever-willing to indulge "his little girl." Initially resistant, my mother eventually yielded after persistent persuasion from my father. He arranged for me to consult with one of the town's top plastic surgeons, who promptly commenced his work on me.

Initially, the surgeries seemed successful. I felt they elevated me to Sarah's level, bringing more friends and attention my way. Yet, Sarah remained unaffected by my transformation and newfound popularity. She carried on as if nothing had changed, but I was resolute in my desire for her to recognize me as her equal in beauty and adoration.

After my third plastic surgery, however, I encountered a grave complication. A surgical error resulted in a slight deformity on my nose, far from what I had envisioned, leaving me seething with anger. "How can I face my friends now?" I pondered in distress. The thought of being seen by my admirers was unbearable. I secluded myself in my room for weeks, oscillating between despair and hope, wishing for my nose to revert to its previous state.

One morning, as I confronted my reflection, the mirror reflected the image the world saw—my brown hair and the facade sculpted by surgery. Yet, it felt dissonant. Beneath the surface lurked a void filled with jealousy, frustration, ambition, and fear. I saw a girl who had strayed from her path.

The realization struck me—I envied Sarah not for her beauty, but because of my own shame, insecurities, and the aspects of myself I loathed but was too fearful to confront. Emboldened by this epiphany, I stepped out the next day, devoid of makeup and pretense, ready to reveal my true self. The reactions were immediate; friends inquired about my changed appearance, some distanced themselves, and others accused me of deceit upon learning of my surgeries. Isolation ensued, and hurtful nicknames like "buck face Lorie" emerged, compounding my sadness and humiliation.

Then, one unexpected day, Sarah knocked on my door. She expressed concern for my well-being and invited me to her room. There, she offered me comfort food and began to play with my hair, admiring its beauty. Despite my protests, she insisted, "It's true." So, she read me this poem celebrating the essence of true beauty:

She's Beautiful
You are the one that beauty sent
    To represent her attributes
At the most rarified event,
    Where beauties vying, bade their bets.

The after report from the fair,
    Which beauty got, was bold and clear:

This virtuous beauty has no peer,
    Her speech, selective and sincere.

Her foes concurred she is quite good,
    Of charms and graces, nothing crude,
Her looks, divine like heav'nly food,
    As for her faults, none to allude.

Her eyes glistened like sparkling mists
    From waterfalls wooed by the sun,
Her smile luscious in awe, persists
    Like blossoms in a summer's morn.

She's beautiful! She's beautiful!
Without a doubt; she's beautiful!

After she finished reading the poem, Sarah beckoned me to the mirror, swept my hair back, and gently said, "See, you are beautiful." In that moment, my insecurities dissolved. I confessed to her my previous resentment, born from her beauty and the adoration she received from everyone. She imparted a profound truth, "Contentment reveals your inner beauty. Never envy others. You possess your own unique beauty, so embrace your true self, and the goodness within you will shine through." Her words moved me to tears, which streamed down my face, soaking my blouse.

With a tender touch, Sarah wiped away my tears. Then, she proposed something unexpected, "Let's walk out together, and you'll show the world the real you." I agreed, heartened by her support.

As we exited the room, it became apparent that word of my time with Sarah had spread. The hallways were lined with students, who I feared would express their disdain. Instead, Sarah's influence transformed the moment. "I want all my friends to embrace Lorie," she declared. One by one, they hugged me, enveloping me in a wave of affection.

Gratitude filled me, and from that day forward, Sarah and I shared a deep friendship.

Yet, despite this turning point, my fixation with the mirror persisted. That winter, upon returning home, my mother introduced me to a psychologist, Dr. Nimble. She was quite attractive herself, and when I inquired about her use of beauty products, she casually replied, "Sometimes." Her flawless skin suggested otherwise, but her focus was strictly professional. During our sessions, she posed a thought-provoking question, "What does your mirror reflect? Does it show external beauty while masking internal envy?" I defensively retorted, "You don't know me." Unfazed, she observed, "I've encountered many who feel they're not perfect enough. No surgery can mend that. The true remedy lies in a heart committed to righteousness." Her words left me speechless, prompting me to abruptly leave the session.

My mother was incensed, so she escorted me back to Dr. Nimble the following week. This time, the doctor suggested, "Let's begin anew. How did this all start?" I recounted a summer in middle school when I proudly wore sandals that showcased my painted toes. A girl's teasing comment about my slightly slanted toes wounded me deeply. When the doctor inquired about my reaction, I admitted that I had harbored thoughts of surgery to correct them, but ultimately, I chose to hide my toes and never spoke to that girl again. Dr. Nimble's question, "Do you realize you're imprisoning yourself by not being able to handle criticism?" struck a nerve. I retorted with frustration, "You can't fathom the pain of being mocked for your appearance." The session ended with the doctor's belief that I suffered from a body dysmorphic disorder, a notion I vehemently rejected, insisting all I desired was to look my best.

In the midst of life's relentless march, my dearest friend Julia embarked on a journey to Nicaragua, seeking to mend the remnants of a past surgery that had left her dreams unfulfilled. It was her third time seeing the same surgeon. Her heart was heavy with hope, yet fate had woven a different path. Tragically, she was swept away from this world too soon, a postoperative infection cruelly snatching her life within the span of a fleeting week. Her absence left a void in my heart, an abyss of sorrow that words could scarcely fill.

That fateful evening, as I stood before the mirror, my reflection staring back at me in its purest form, an epiphany washed over me like a gentle wave. For the first time, I saw beauty in my untouched visage, a beauty that had always been there, yet I had been blind to it. The years I had spent entangled in a web of self-doubt and anxiety over my appearance now seemed like a distant, inconsequential memory.

Perhaps it was Julia's untimely departure that served as a piercing siren, a wake-up call that resonated deep within my soul. With newfound clarity, I turned to my mother, my voice steady and sure, and declared that the endless cycle of appointments with Dr. Nimble was no longer necessary. For I had discovered the remedy not in the sterile rooms of clinics, but within the sanctuary of my own heart.

13

The Necklace

It was 2015, and Janet Cole, nineteen years old, was living with her father, Jerry. Autumn had arrived, and the vast foliage was a testament to nature's quest for beauty. The leaves, in their rusty, copper-like colors and bright, flame-like hues, formed the backdrop of the quaint town in northern Kansas where they resided. The air was crisp and filled with the scent of pine and damp earth, a refreshing change from the summer's heat. As the days grew shorter, the golden light of the afternoon sun filtered through the canopy, casting a warm glow that seemed to set the world alight with an amber radiance. The gentle rustling of the leaves created a concerto of whispers, a reminder that even as they fell, they gave life to the forest floor below.

This season of harvest was a time for reflection, a period to ponder the bounties of life and to find joy in simplicity. It was a time when the heart grew fonder of the little marvels that often went unnoticed, a time to cherish the ephemeral beauty of the world transforming before her eyes.

By all accounts, they were happy; Janet was her daddy's girl. She had lived with her father since she was eleven, following her parents' divorce. Despite living apart, her parents got along quite well. In fact, Jerry often remarked that they were more amicable separated than together. Janet frequently visited her mother, Juliet, in Falls City, a small enclave in southeastern Nebraska.

That evening, as the shadows lengthened and the world quieted, Janet's heart was gripped by a chill that went deeper than the autumn air. The call from her brother was a thunderclap in the calm of her daily life, shattering the peace with three words: "Mum is missing." The words echoed, a relentless refrain that filled her thoughts, leaving no room for the beauty that once brought her solace.

The journey to Falls City became a pilgrimage of anxiety, each mile a stretch of uncertainty. The autumnal beauty that unfolded outside the car window was lost on Janet, her mind a turbulent sea of worry and fear. She sought answers from Jerry, grasping for any thread of hope, but his assurances felt like whispers against a storm.

Their arrival at the Falls City police station at 2 p.m. was a descent into reality, the questions a probe into the unknown. Jerry's words to the officers were a flood of information, an attempt to fill the void where Juliet should be.

As days turned into weeks, the rumors swirled like leaves in the wind, each one a flicker of suspicion that faded as quickly as it appeared. The search through the woods was a quest for closure, the absence of evidence a silent scream in the quiet of the forest.

The service at the church was a confluence of grief and love, a gathering of souls united in loss. The chief of police's regret was a cold comfort, his promise a faint beacon in the fog of their despair. The pastor's words were a balm, yet they could not seal the cracks in their broken hearts.

The tree planted in Juliet's honor was a living memorial, the purple ribbon a symbol of her spirit—vibrant and enduring. It was a promise to remember, to hold her essence in the roots of their lives.

On the return journey, as Janet awoke to the medley of flowers on the farms they passed, it was as if the world had donned Juliet's favorite hues. The sight of her mother, ethereal atop the blooms, was a vision of peace, a whisper from beyond that love transcends all boundaries.

Jerry's words, "your mum is with us, and she will always be with us," were a gentle anchor, a reminder that Juliet's influence would be permanently interlaced with the very essence of their being. In the dance of the lilacs and asters, in the purple that painted the horizon, Janet found a silent message—a mother's love is an eternal embrace, a comforting presence in the garden of memories they carry within.

Back in the sanctuary of her own home, Janet felt the whispers of unease stirring within her. The walls that once promised solitude now echoed with the persistence of her thoughts, each one a silent echo of her mother's unsolved case. It was this restlessness that propelled her towards a new beginning, a shift in the tides of her life that led her to Falls City in a town about twenty miles from her mother's home.

In the quiet embrace of the countryside, just beyond the outskirts of Falls City, Janet found solace in a quaint house nestled on a dusty, unpaved road. It was there she encountered James Bradford, a kind-hearted bachelor shadowed by the loss of his parents. An unspoken bond quickly formed between them, as James's generous spirit saw him assisting Janet with the smallest of tasks, his presence a balm to her solitude.

As twilight painted the sky, the melodic strumming of James's guitar and his soulful voice, carrying tunes of love and longing, would drift through the air. His renditions of beloved songs became a nightly serenade to Janet's aching heart. Despite the growing affection in his heart, Janet maintained a guarded distance, her soul still shrouded in the sorrow of her mother's untimely departure from this world.

Months of tireless inquiries with the authorities yielded no solace for Janet, and with a heavy heart, she chose to step out from under the pall of her grief. Embracing the promise of new beginnings, she made a silent vow to let the shadows of the past rest, sealing away the pain of her mother's demise in a corner of her heart, never to be spoken of again.

Undeterred by her reticence, James persisted in his courtship. Under the moon's gentle glow, he would serenade Janet with heartfelt love ballads, each note floating up to her window—a wordless confession of his affection. Then, one fateful evening, as Janet retreated to the sanctuary of her bedroom, a cry from James shattered the stillness: her kitchen was ablaze. With no thought for his own safety, James leaped into action, battling the flames with fierce determination. By the time the fire brigade arrived, he had subdued the inferno, saving Janet's cherished home from ruin. The aftermath left Janet reeling—her mind was adamant that she had extinguished every appliance. Yet, the fire's mysterious origin remained unsolved, even after the fire department's scrutiny. James's account, however, seemed to quell their queries. Overwhelmed by his heroism, Janet's heart began to thaw, and gratitude blossomed into affection.

As the summer sun heralded the season of warmth, James whisked Janet away to a serene lake for their inaugural date. There, amidst forty sprawling acres of nature's canvas, they found a secluded haven, alive with the promise of adventure and tranquility. Anglers dotted the landscape, reveling in the lake's bountiful offerings. Amidst the throng of nature enthusiasts, Janet and James found solace in each other's company, the summer breeze caressing their skin, the air fragrant with the scent of wildflowers. That evening, as they journeyed back, they paused at a cozy diner, its ambiance a blend of nostalgia and comfort. There, they indulged in the smoky flavors of barbecued brisket and ribs, the sweetness of cornbread, and the earthy tones of collard greens, all washed down with the shared experience of a cold beer.

On their ensuing date, James led Janet to his time-honored log cabin for a weekend retreat, about thirty miles from the hum of their town. Cradled in nature's tender hold, the cabin—a legacy of James' father—stood as an endearing relic, its spruce walls whispering tales of yesteryears. Despite its age, the cabin was a bastion of comfort, complete with the luxuries of modernity, such as running water and electricity. Together, they basked in the ensemble of nature: birds' lilting songs and the leaves' gentle rustle, as if nature itself was celebrating their union.

As the bond between them deepened, James peeled back the layers of his past. He laid bare his battles with addiction, the days swallowed by the false euphoria of cocaine, and the salvation he found in therapy and the strums of his guitar. Janet's heart burgeoned with empathy, her affection for the man before her—resilient and reborn—growing stronger, kindling hope for a shared horizon.

Their exploration took them across the five-acre expanse, where they discovered towering maple trees guarding over stone mounds, like ancient guards. James revealed his ritual of clearing the land's stones, each stack a monument to perseverance. Janet, moved by the symbolism, joined him in this act of creation, their stones of effort joining the silent chorus under the maples. As twilight beckoned, they retreated to the cabin's warm embrace, their evening spent in shared meals and intimate conversation, each moment a precious thread in the loom of their burgeoning love.

As dawn broke the next day, Janet and James journeyed back to the rhythm of town life. With hearts full of lingering warmth from their idyllic retreat, they bid each other farewell. Janet's words were steeped in appreciation for the unforgettable weekend, and together, they eagerly anticipated their next escape to the cabin.

Come Monday evening, the air was once again filled with the tender strains of James's guitar. This time, his lyrics held a new intimacy, Janet's name woven into each verse. The melody, a familiar caress, beckoned her to the window. There, she found herself swaying to the rhythm, her laughter mingling with the night as James infused humor into his serenade. It was a dance of joy and connection, a ritual that cradled them into the night.

On Thursday's gentle morning, a sight stirred Janet's curiosity—a police officer departing from James's abode. Later, fueled by concern, she sought answers. James recounted the morning's drama: an alarm triggered without cause, the swift arrival of the authorities. It was a testament to the monitoring company's watchful eye, he said, a reassurance that left him grateful for their protective gaze.

The weekend beckoned, and with it, Janet and James found themselves once again at the secluded cabin, a place that was quickly becoming their shared refuge. They meandered through the yard, the tranquility of nature enveloping them, as they continued their labor of love— clearing the stones. It was during this peaceful interlude that Janet's hand instinctively reached for her neck, her complexion turning ashen. "Oh dear, I've lost my brooch," she murmured, her voice a fragile echo of distress. James offered to search for it, but Janet, with a laugh that didn't quite reach her eyes, brushed off the loss, claiming the brooch's monetary insignificance.

Yet, unbeknownst to James, the brooch was a tangible connection to Janet's mother—a memento of love and loss. In her heart, Janet wrestled with the decision to release this last vestige of her mother, striving to adhere to her vow of looking forward, not back.

As they neared the cabin, James, ever the beacon of new experiences, proposed an adventure to his treehouse. Janet's response was a burst of genuine enthusiasm. They ascended to the quaint structure, its eight-by-eight-foot space a testament to simpler times, albeit marred by the telltale signs of neglect—a musty odor and a roof beam slightly askew, betraying its battle with the elements.

"Wait here while I get a hammer to fix this beam," James said, his voice steady with resolve. Janet, left alone with the whispers of the past, began to explore the treehouse's nooks and crannies. It was then, in a hidden hollow, that she uncovered a necklace shrouded in soft white paper—a star-shaped opal pendant that mirrored the one her mother cherished, the very one she donned on the day she vanished. A cold tide of horror surged through Janet, the chilling realization dawning upon her—could the man she was growing to love be entwined with her mother's disappearance? The question hung in the air, heavy and ominous: Was her own life in peril?

Janet stood frozen, her mouth agape and eyes as wide as a startled deer caught in the glare of oncoming headlights. She snapped her mouth shut, teeth clenching in a silent scream, her pulse thundering in her ears. Despite the turmoil churning within, she managed to cloak herself in a veneer of calm. When James's gaze met hers, the necklace in her trembling hands, he spoke with a nonchalance that belied the gravity of the find, "I see you've discovered my hidden treasures. Feel free to claim it as your own." His words were a balm, yet beneath the surface, suspicion gnawed at her. His tale of familial lineage for the necklace rang hollow, and as she clasped it around her neck, a visceral connection to her mother surged through her, both comforting and haunting.

As the day bled into twilight and James put the finishing touches on his handiwork, Janet clutched at her abdomen, feigning a sudden ailment. "I need to use the bathroom. I think my period has started," she murmured, her voice laced with urgency. They descended from their lofty perch, and she hastened to the sanctuary of the bathroom. In a moment of desperate ingenuity, she drew her own blood, staining the vanity as a silent testament to her presence—a breadcrumb trail for those who might search for her. She called out to James, her voice quivering with feigned distress, requesting tampons. He offered to accompany her, but she insisted on solitude, promising a swift return. With a heart racing against time, she slipped into the night's embrace, commandeering his vehicle, and set a course for the police station, where Officer Mulcahy awaited—a beacon of hope in unraveling the mystery of her mother's fate.

By a stroke of fate, Detective Mulcahy and his team were present when Janet burst through the precinct doors, her hands clutching the opal necklace and a photograph of her mother adorned in the same piece. The air crackled with urgency as the SWAT team was summoned, and the chilling truth unfurled—James had long been a shadowy figure in the investigation of her mother's disappearance. Betrayal seared through Janet as she realized the detectives' silence had shrouded her in ignorance. Her confrontation with them was a tempest of fury and disbelief.

As the SWAT team stealthily converged upon the cabin, James, ensnared in his own oblivion, reached out to Janet by phone. Her response was a mixture of lies, concocted to keep him unsuspecting. Within heartbeats, the silence of the night was shattered by the police's decisive entry, and James was ensnared in the arms of justice.

In the sterile glow of the interrogation room, a silent ballet of gazes between James and Janet spoke volumes—his dawning awareness of her betrayal, her steely resolve. Hours ticked by, with James steadfastly proclaiming the necklace's lineage within his family. Yet, spurred by Janet's harrowing account, the police unleashed their hounds of justice upon the cabin grounds. Night's cloak fell too soon, halting their search, leaving James to the company of his thoughts in the cold embrace of a cell, as dawn's light promised revelations.

As the first light of dawn painted the sky in hues of orange and pink, the hounds, with their keen senses, alerted to the somber stone mounds. The air was thick with anticipation as the excavation commenced. Janet stood there, a silent sentinel, her eyes wide with a mix of fear and hope, as the officers carefully unearthed three bodies from their earthen tomb.

Merely three feet from the grave, glinting in the morning light, lay the brooch Janet had thought forever lost. It was a haunting reminder of a walk taken, a memory shared with James on these very grounds. With trembling hands, she confirmed to the officers that the brooch was indeed hers, a tangible piece of the past now resurfaced.

Amidst the unearthed, one body was poignantly familiar. The clothing, the personal effects—it was unmistakably her mother. The revelation pierced Janet's heart like a shard of ice. The other two, young women from a neighboring county, remained shrouded in mystery, their stories untold.

The investigation extended its reach to the tree house, that once innocent haven now yielding more secrets in the form of collected items.

When confronted with the mounting evidence, James's facade crumbled. He confessed to the heinous acts, his mind and soul marred by cocaine-fueled frenzies. In a cruel twist of fate, he had never linked Janet to her mother, their relationship a barren landscape, devoid of shared history or affection.

In the wake of tragedy, Janet and her family sought solace in ritual, gathering in the local church to bid a final, tearful farewell to her mother. It was a ceremony steeped in sorrow, yet it offered a glimmer of closure, a chance to lay to rest more than just a beloved figure—a chance to bury the anguish and the torment that had gripped their lives. She read this poem in honor of her mum:

Eternal Rest, Beloved Mother

You're gone too soon, dear mother,
   May you with saints be blessed,
In heav'n, God's awesome wonder
   Will grant you peaceful rest.

You will be missed, dear mother;
   Your beauty and your zest,
Your smiles with joys and laughter,
   You'll share with heaven's best.

Your love we'll keep, dear mother
   In all we say and do,
No life's hardship will ever,
   Make us dishonor you.

The things you taught, dear mother,
   In life will get us through;
To forgive one another,
   And live a life's that's true.

Tis lonely here, dear mother,
   A void your absence makes,
Yet, we know God, our Father
   Loves best the saints he takes.

As the final notes of the service faded into a profound silence, Janet stood enveloped in the warmth of shared sorrow and love. The weight of her mother's absence was a silent companion, yet in the solace of expression, she found a glimmer of peace. Her mother's death, a wound time could never fully heal, had become a part of her, a bittersweet reminder of the fragility of life and the enduring strength of love. In the echoes of her words, in the gentle embrace of her community, Janet discovered a resilient hope—a beacon in the darkness. It was a belief, steadfast and unwavering, that through the cherished legacy of her mother's spirit, she could continue to love, to learn, and to live. With a heart brimming with gratitude for the precious, fleeting moments they shared, Janet stepped forward into the future, carrying with her the eternal flame of her mother's memory—a guiding light on the path of healing and renewal.

14

The Oak Tree

In 2005, within a quiet enclave of Jupiter, Florida, Joanna Johnson and Sam Carmichael found themselves caught in a family feud. Their parents, embroiled in a bitter dispute over a property line, forbade them from speaking to each other. The bone of contention was a majestic oak tree that stood between their homes, with both families claiming it as their own.

Each family, employing the same contractor, erected a six-foot tall, clay brick privacy fence along their property's edge. The fences, however, stopped short of the oak tree—a testament to the stubbornness of both parties. It was a ludicrous expenditure, driven by the fragile egos of the patriarchs, who refused to share the tree's benefits. The stalemate persisted until a judge could rule on the matter, as previous arbitration efforts had failed.

Tom Johnson, Joanna's father, was a tall, lean man with a penchant for hunting and an even greater fondness for his gun collection. He prided himself on being an "old school gentleman," making unilateral decisions for his family. Yet, his actions often contradicted his proclaimed values.

Patrick Carmichael, Sam's father, stood out with his tall, handsome stature and unassuming demeanor. An insurance salesman by trade, he led his family with a gentle hand. Both families were regular churchgoers, with Joanna's mother teaching Sunday school.

As the dispute raged on, teenagers Joanna and Sam communicated silently through the gaps in the fence. Joanna was drawn to Sam's piercing blue eyes, which, despite their apparent lack of emotion, intrigued her. Sam, bearing a strong resemblance to his father, had the commanding presence of a TV news anchor.

Sam was equally captivated by Joanna's hazel eyes and the warmth they occasionally betrayed. Their silent exchanges, filled with longing and curiosity, continued unabated, each lost in the depths of the other's gaze.

As the summer sun cast long shadows across the Johnson and Carmichael yards, the oak tree planted by a previous owner who owned both properties stood silently at the heart of the dispute—a living monument to the families' shared history and divided present. It was beneath this very tree that Joanna and Sam, separated by more than just a fence, exchanged secret glances filled with longing and unspoken promises.

After graduating from high school, Joanna and Sam found themselves walking the same college paths. Their acquaintance blossomed into friendship, thanks to a mutual friend, Katie Detweiler, who was Sam's study partner. What began as casual flirtations and nervous compliments soon evolved into a deep connection. Their playful banter gave way to sincere admiration, and love took root. They shared letters, meals, and long walks, their hands intertwined amidst the verdant college grounds.

Both excelled academically, with Sam pursuing psychology and Joanna aiming to inspire young minds as a grade school teacher. They often discussed their families' ongoing dispute, dismissing it with laughter and vowing to end the senseless feud.

In one heartfelt letter, Joanna wrote:

"Sam, my dear, you are love personified amidst life's trials. In moments of pain and fear, my faith in you is unwavering. My love for you is as eternal as the sun, as pure as snow on a mountain peak, and as free-flowing as a river seeking the sea—and you are that sea. I am yours, completely and forever."

Sam's response echoed her sentiments:

"Joanna, my heart, you are my hope and joy; the treasure I cherish. You dwell in my heart, as I do in yours, trusting in our bond. Together, we'll weather any storm, always seeking the rainbow or the dawn of a new day, regardless of our parents' views."

On one occasion, the two budding lovers composed a poem together, taking turns writing each line. The poem reads:

Daring To Thrive

Midst disdain, our love dares to thrive,
A tender bloom, primed to survive.
    Our parents' scorn, may rage and roar,
    We've found a love that's bound to soar.

Gainst the tide of their bitter feud,
Our hearts unite, in fortitude;
    For love, it knows no bounds nor hate,
    It leaps and soars, not hesitate.

Our whispered vows are seeds in ground,
In spite of hate, take root, profound.
    Our love, a silent flame, burns bright,
    Guiding us through the darkest night.

So let them glare, in time they'll see,
Our love is strong, it's meant to be.
    Despite the odds, our souls entwine,
    A tribute to a love divine.

As their relationship deepened, they faced the challenge of their families' animosity. Yet, their love, like the oak tree, remained steadfast—a symbol of hope in the midst of conflict.

While Joanna and Sam were away at college, the acrimony between their families persisted. One afternoon, a heated argument erupted, with words as sharp as arrows flying across the property line, each carrying years of accumulated bitterness. Tom, with the precision of a hunter, aimed his words carefully, each one heavy with the weight of his convictions. Patrick, though less accustomed to confrontation, stood his ground, his voice steady with the resolve of a man protecting his family's legacy.

The escalation was swift, the air crackling with the tension of an impending storm. Yet, it was the wisdom of their wives, born from years of quiet observation and understanding, that calmed the rising tempest. With hearts racing and breaths held, they intervened, their words serving not as weapons but as shields against the folly of pride.

Three weeks later, the skies wept gentle tears, and nature left its indelible mark—a hefty limb from the disputed oak tree lay across the fence bridging the gap, a poignant reminder of the fragility of life. It seemed almost a divine intervention, a silent plea for the two families to mend the rift and heal the wounds of enmity that had festered for too long. Patrick, with the growl of a chainsaw piercing the tranquil morning, set to work on the fallen wood. The noise, a harsh intruder upon the day's calm, drew Tom out, his face contorted into a familiar scowl, a visage of the bitterness that had long shadowed their shared history.

"What do you think you're doing?" Tom barked over the din, his voice struggling to rise above the chainsaw's roar.

Patrick turned off the engine, and the sudden silence was heavy with tension. "Just cleaning up what the storm left behind," he replied, his tone even, though his jaw was tight.

The momentary retreat was short-lived; they returned armed—not with understanding, but with weapons mirroring their escalating rage. Tom, adept with firearms, brandished a shotgun, while Patrick, less experienced, clutched a newly acquired handgun.

Their wives, sensing the imminent danger, rushed outside. With a blend of fear and determination, they implored their husbands to stand down. "Enough," they declared in unison, their voices merging like the branches of the oak above them. "This ends now, for the sake of our children and the peace of this place we all call home."

In the city's heart, far removed from suburban disputes, Joanna and Sam found refuge in their shared aspirations and intimate confessions. Their connection, shaped by the shadows of familial conflict, strengthened with each day. Hand in hand, they strolled through the college's verdant grounds, their laughter blending with the rustling leaves—a symphony of hope against a backdrop of discord.

The summer of 2008 marked a turning point in their love story. Leaving the college corridors behind, Joanna and Sam staged a daring act of solidarity beneath the oak tree's expansive limbs. The cookout was more than a gathering—it was a challenge to the unspoken edicts that had long dictated their families' dealings. Joanna arranged her father's table under the tree, while Sam set up his father's grill. Together, they began to cook, their actions defying the tacit rules of their parents' no-man's-land. The aroma of grilled food and the cadence of laughter lured their fathers to the scene, their faces etched with bewilderment and lingering resentment.

Sam's father, taken aback, confronted his son. Joanna's parents, upon seeing the dispute, were met with her composed affirmation of love for Sam—a love they had unknowingly nurtured through letters to their daughter, unaware that her beloved was Sam Carmichael. Feeling deceived, the tension escalated, but Joanna's firm voice sliced through the discord, her declaration resonating with defiance and affection.

"Dad, this must end," she implored, her gaze unwavering. "Our love isn't the adversary."

As dusk approached and the parents retreated, Joanna and Sam reflected on their audacious stance. Seated in the growing shadows, their shared silence spoke volumes of their determination. They had opted for love over lineage, envisioning a future unmarred by the walls of acrimony. Aware of the challenges ahead, they remained resolute, their love a fortress against adversity. Embracing, they exchanged whispers of love, tidied the area, and departed, their spirits buoyed by the triumph of unity.

The morning after their bold cookout, both families received a stern letter from Judge Lithgow, who had recently taken over their fence dispute case. The letter read:

"It is with great disappointment that I address this trivial matter before the court. Your persistent stubbornness has led me to consider imposing a fine for the unnecessary burden you've placed upon our legal system. Alternatively, I may issue a unique sentence that forces you into close quarters at the very fence that divides you. I urge you to resolve this petty quarrel, lest you leave me no choice but to enact the aforementioned consequences."

Judge Lithgow, familiar with both families, hoped his direct appeal would prompt a peaceful resolution. His involvement came at the recommendation of a colleague who knew of his personal connection to the families.

In response, the parents convened the following week to mend their rift. They extended heartfelt apologies for past grievances and reached out to Judge Lithgow, informing him of their decision to co-own the tree and requesting the dismissal of the case.

United by Joanna and Sam's example, the families grew closer. They began hosting joint dinners, sharing an array of dishes and homemade beverages. Sam's mother, renowned for her culinary skills, delighted everyone with her diverse recipes. Tom and Patrick bonded over baseball, watching games together and attending Florida's Major League spring training.

One evening, over drinks at a local bar, the two patriarchs reflected on their past animosity. They marveled at the absurdity of fighting over a tree that now symbolized their shared bond. Acknowledging their previous folly, they agreed that both had been irrational, though each playfully claimed the other more so. Now, they could laugh about the feud that once seemed so dire.

Three years after the fence dispute, under the boughs of the once-contested oak tree, Sam and Joanna vowed to forge a shared future. Surrounded by friends and family, they stood where discord once reigned, now a place of unity and love. Judge Lithgow, who had witnessed the families' journey from conflict to reconciliation, officiated the ceremony.

In his opening remarks, Judge Lithgow reflected on the transformation before him. "Today," he began, "we gather not just to witness the union of two individuals, but to celebrate the mending of bonds once frayed by strife. This oak tree, once a symbol of division, now stands as a testament to the enduring power of love over discord."

He continued, "As we join these families under its canopy, we are reminded that love's roots can weather the storms of anger and hatred. Today, the love between Joanna and Sam blossoms, a living proof that unity can triumph over division."

The judge then lightened the mood with a jest, "Let us all embrace moderation today—especially with the spirits. Remember, if you overindulge, ensure you have a ride home, lest the law becomes your unintended host for the evening." His words drew laughter and nods of agreement from the gathering.

As the ceremony concluded, the laughter and joyous conversations echoed through the branches, a harmonious chorus that celebrated the beginning of a new chapter for two families, united at last.

As Judge Lithgow concluded his remarks, Joanna and Sam reflected on how their love had indeed transformed their once-divided families. The wedding reception was a joyous affair, with friends and family reveling in the celebration. True to their journey, the couple had some of the food grilled beneath the oak tree, symbolizing the unity they had fostered.

Their honeymoon in the Caribbean marked their first venture outside the United States. They immersed themselves in the vibrant scenery, connected with locals, and savored the flavors of dishes like jerk chicken. By chance, they encountered friends celebrating their own anniversary at the same resort, adding to the serendipity of their trip.

Back home, Katie Detweiler, now a television journalist, interviewed them beneath the oak tree. The segment revealed the stubbornness of their parents and showcased the couple's loving resolve. Viewers were touched by the story, praising Joanna and Sam for their compassion and strength.

When asked for their final thoughts, Joanna said, "Our love stands as a beacon for families and neighbors in conflict, a reminder to never erect barriers against love and understanding. Instead, we should open our hearts to compromise, love, and peace. Just as there are many shades of oak trees, there is room for all to share in their shelter."

Katie concluded the interview with a nod to Joanna's words, "As you've heard, there are plenty of oak trees for us all to enjoy together."

15

The Old Man and The Ocean

James Sung's existence was a mosaic of seclusion, intricately pieced together with strands of tenacity and the raw allure of the natural world. Nestled close to the seashore, his humble abode in the remote village of Fresco on the island of Sumatra was a testament to the untouched splendor of the world. The rugged mountain cliffs stood as silent guardians over this slice of paradise, a place where the industrial revolution's touch had yet to mar the landscape, preserving a glimpse of the earth's pristine past.

Fresco, a village cradled in the embrace of Sumatra's natural grandeur, is a canvas of vibrant greens and deep blues. Imagine a place where the air is filled with the scent of salt and earth, where the horizon is a dance of land meeting sea. The landscape is a masterpiece of nature's finest elements: lush, verdant jungles that host a myriad of life, their canopies painting dappled shadows on the earth below.

The coastline is a masterpiece of white sandy beaches, fringed by the gentle sway of coconut palms, their fronds whispering secrets to the ocean breeze. The sea itself is a dazzling array of blues, from the palest aquamarine to the deepest sapphire, reflecting the mood of the sky above. It is here that the waves caress the shore with tender laps, only to retreat back into the vast, open arms of the Indian Ocean.

Inland, the terrain rises gently at first, into rolling hills that boast a patchwork of rice paddies and vegetable gardens, meticulously tended by the villagers. These fields are a testament to the symbiotic relationship between man and nature, where every plant and every harvest is a shared victory.

As one ventures further, the hills ascend into rugged mountain cliffs, standing as stoic guardians over the village. These cliffs are adorned with a variety of mosses and ferns, and waterfalls cascade down their faces like liquid silver, feeding into crystal-clear streams that meander through the village.

The heart of Fresco is its single dirt road, a lifeline that weaves through the village, lined with modest homes made of bamboo and thatch. This road tells a story of simplicity and connection, a path well-traveled by barefoot children and elders alike, each step a testament to the enduring spirit of the community.

At night, the landscape transforms as the sky becomes a canvas for the stars, unmarred by the light pollution of distant cities. The constellations tell ancient tales, while the gentle glow of fireflies punctuates the darkness, creating a serene and enchanting atmosphere.

This is Fresco, a place where time seems to stand still, where the beauty of the earth is preserved, and where the rhythm of life moves to the ancient and enduring beat of nature's drum.

Loneliness was not always the companion of Mr. Sung. Once surrounded by the warmth of a family, with a wife and two daughters, he toiled the land, living a life of subsistence agriculture. But fate, with its cruel twists, brought a hurricane that ravaged their farm, a storm that tested their very souls. And then, the tsunami—a monstrous wave that tore through the village on an otherwise tranquil Thursday morning, just as his family savored a breakfast of eggs and tropical fruits. The animals, sensing the impending doom, scattered in panic. In moments, Sung's world was engulfed by the relentless sea, his home and heart swept away as he clung desperately to a tree branch, the last vestige of his former life.

Discovered unconscious days later, the village survivors nursed him back to health over four grueling months. With newfound strength, he returned to the ruins of his home, erecting a modest mud house on the scarred land. There, amidst the solitude, he would sometimes succumb to the weight of his memories, tears flowing for the family he lost. Yet, he understood the harshness of life and strove to move beyond the shadows of his tragedy.

Each day, Sung greeted the dawn with a routine that tethered him to life: gathering firewood, tending to his garden, and venturing to the ocean's edge in hopes of a bountiful catch. On one particularly sweltering afternoon, as the sun beamed down with an almost approving glow, he stumbled upon a large striped bass, floundering on the shore, desperate to return to the life-giving embrace of the sea. The sight of the struggling creature stirred something within him—a recognition of shared vulnerability. In an act of compassion, he aided the bass back into the ocean, forsaking his easy meal for the life of another.

That evening, as he returned to his hut empty-handed, the pangs of hunger were overshadowed by a profound sense of gratitude. He had chosen mercy over necessity, and though his dinner table bore only fruits and legumes, his spirit was nourished by the act of kindness. As night fell, Sung lay in his bed, the echoes of the day's lesson whispering through his mind: even in the depths of solitude, there exists the capacity for profound connection and the enduring hope of redemption.

Two days after his act of kindness, James Sung returned to the seashore, his fishing gear in hand, his heart heavy with the day's expectations. The ocean, a vast expanse of memories and sustenance, lay before him, its waves whispering tales of both generosity and cruelty. As he prepared for his humble quest for dinner, he noticed three fish, their scales glinting in the sun, struggling against the sandy prison that the retreating tide had left them in. Their frantic movements tugged at Sung's conscience, echoing his own struggles against the merciless whims of nature.

He recalled the moment, not long past, when he had faced a similar choice. To take what the sea offered or to grant mercy to its creatures. With a resolve softened by empathy, he chose once again to release them into the ocean. The first two fish found their freedom with ease, slipping back into the water as if they understood his silent apology. The third, however, seemed to resist, slipping from his grasp twice, as if testing his commitment to this act of compassion. On his third attempt, Sung's determination was rewarded, and the fish returned to its home, leaving him with a sense of bittersweet victory.

As he stood there, contemplating the ebb and flow of life, his gaze fell upon an unexpected treasure—a sealed bottle, cradled by the grains of sand stands mute vigil over an enigmatic secret it harbors.

Curiosity piqued, he retrieved the bottle, its contents a mystery that would unfold in due time.

Fortune smiled upon Sung that day, as the sea yielded two Snappers to his line. With a heart grateful for the ocean's gifts and the lives he had spared, he returned to his humble abode. That evening, as he savored his meal of broiled snapper, complemented by the fresh bounty of his garden, he pondered the sealed message that lay beside him.

The following day, curiosity overcame Sung, and he broke the seal of the bottle to reveal its secret—a note, its words a puzzle to his untrained eyes. Seeking understanding, he turned to a fellow villager, a man who had once pulled him from the clutches of despair. Together, they puzzled over the cryptic message, its meaning just beyond their grasp. It was decided—a journey to the city of Bongboi was in order, in search of someone who could unlock the words' secrets.

In Bongboi, they found Jane Lee, a beacon of knowledge who had once called their village home and a childhood acquaintance of Sung's youngest daughter. With gentle patience, she deciphered the note's message: "If you find this bottle, consider yourself fortunate. God, the Maker is ready to bless you." Skepticism and wonder danced in her eyes as she contemplated the note's intent. Was it a jest, or something more? She urged the men to call the number, to unravel the mystery that the sea had presented them.

Together, they approached a payphone, the gateway to answers. Jane, with a spark of curiosity igniting her own spirit, dialed the number. The voice that answered was a mystery, its owner hidden behind the veil of anonymity. Yet, as the conversation unfolded, a connection was made. The voice sought the man who had plucked the message from the ocean's grasp—James Sung.

A meeting was arranged, a date set, and the promise of an encounter that could change everything hung in the air. As they parted ways, Sung felt the stirrings of hope, a feeling that had become a stranger to him. Perhaps the ocean, with its boundless sagacity, had presented him with a fresh course, an opportunity to craft a new narrative in the mosaic of his existence.

Three months had passed since the message in a bottle had made its way into the lives of James Sung and his friend, Park. On a crisp Monday morning, as autumn adorned the world in hues of amber and gold, they embarked on a journey that seemed as uncertain as the changing leaves. The boat that carried them from Fresco to Bongboi seemed to float on a sea of questions—was this a wild goose chase, a cruel joke played by fate? Yet, as they glided across the strait, the beauty of nature's autumnal display unfurled before them, igniting a spark of hope in their hearts.

In Bongboi, they were met by Jane and an unassuming man whose gentle demeanor belied his noble lineage. He introduced himself as Prince Balzer of Saipon, a realm a thousand miles from their own. His story was one of survival against the odds. He was born with sickle cell anemia and given only a few months to live by doctors. His life, deemed too fragile to endure, was sustained by what he believed to be divine grace. On his wedding day, he had vowed to extend this grace to another, casting a message into the sea's vast unknown, promising a blessing to its finder.

The revelation of the message's true meaning sent waves of elation crashing over Sung and Park. The prince's generosity was as vast as the ocean itself—one hundred thousand British pounds and an invitation to a world beyond their wildest dreams. Overwhelmed by the turn of events, tears streamed down their faces, a mixture of joy and disbelief.

Before parting, Prince Balzer, with a touch of regal kindness, clothed them in new garments and bestowed upon them a sum for their travels. An invitation to his palace in Saipon was extended, a promise of an adventure that lay just over the horizon.

Returning to Fresco, the men shared their fortune with the village, their tale as captivating as the sea from which it sprang. Skepticism and wonder mingled among the villagers, some doubting, others inspired to seek their own bottled messages along the shore.

The day of departure arrived, and the village united in a heartfelt send-off, their prayers and well-wishes a gentle breeze at the backs of Sung and Park. The journey to Saipon was a flight into a new chapter, a leap into a fairytale.

Saipon greeted them with open arms and a red carpet, a welcome befitting heroes of lore. They were whisked away to the prince's residence, where the princess awaited, her joy a radiant beacon. That evening, they dined with the king, Prince Balzer's father, whose graciousness knew no bounds. A ball in their honor was announced, a celebration of their incredible journey.

As the day of the ball dawned, the visitors were treated to a breakfast fit for kings, a stark contrast to their simple village fare. And as night descended, only the crescent moon bore witness to the secrets about to unfold. The path to the palace was a river of light, bamboo torches flickering like stars fallen to earth, guiding them to a night of enchantment.

Inside the palace, the splendor was breathtaking. Gilded mirrors reflected the joy of the moment, ornate cornices whispered tales of grandeur, and the portraits of kings and queens past watched over the dance hall with silent approval. For Sung and Park, this was more than a ball—it was a dance with destiny, a waltz with the wonders of a world they had never dared to imagine.

The ceremony was steeped in a silence so profound it seemed to cradle the very words of the king as he stood before the assembly, his voice a tender echo of gratitude that filled the space with its resonance. He spoke not just as a monarch, but as a father profoundly touched by the grace that had spared his son from the clutches of death. His words were a balm, soothing the hearts of all who listened, as he welcomed the special guests with a warmth that melted the formalities of the court.

As he introduced Jane Lee, Jay Park, and James Sung, there was a palpable sense of anticipation, a collective breath held as the story of their extraordinary journey to the palace was about to be unveiled. But in the midst of this, a singular cry cut through the anticipation—a cry that seemed to vibrate with the very essence of longing and love. "Papa," it called, a word so simple yet laden with the weight of a thousand emotions, a word that reached into the depths of James Sung's being, stirring memories long buried beneath the waves of time.

It was a voice that Sung had carried within him, a haunting melody that had played over in his mind through the darkest nights—the voice of his daughter, Sun Yi. The very same voice that had been snatched away by the merciless sea, now returned to him in a moment of surreal serendipity.

Time itself seemed to bow to the gravity of their reunion, pausing as Sung turned to behold the sight he had never dared to hope for—Sun Yi, not a specter of the past, but flesh and blood, alive and reaching out to him. Their eyes met across the expanse of the ballroom, a silent conversation of souls that had been severed and now sought each other with a desperation that transcended words.

As they came together, the distance of years and heartache collapsed into the singularity of their embrace. Tears, those silent harbingers of joy and sorrow, streamed down their faces, unrestrained. They wept not just for the pain of separation, but for the overwhelming joy of being reunited. Their bond, it seemed, was not one that could be broken by time or tragedy. It was a bond forged in love, tempered by loss, and now, in this moment of miraculous reunion, it shone with a purity that illuminated the entire room.

The crowd, witnesses to this intimate weave of human emotion, felt their own hearts swell with empathy. For in the embrace of father and daughter, in the tears they shared and the silent strength of their hold, there was a message that resonated with every soul present: Love endures. Love transcends. Love reunites. And in that truth, there is a beauty that outshines even the grandeur of palaces and the pomp of ceremonies. It is the beauty of the human heart, relentless in its capacity to heal, and to love again.

Sun Yi recounted her harrowing tale of survival during the tsunami, of being plucked from the ocean's grasp by a fishing vessel and finding a new life in the kingdom of Saipon. She spoke of her marriage to Bila, Prince Balzer's distant cousin, and the search for her father that had come up empty while he lay in a coma's silent grip. She had met Bila at a concert held at the school where she taught.

The guests, caught in the whirlwind of emotion, watched with tear-filled eyes as the stoic king himself was moved to tears by the poignant scene. As the night progressed, Sung was embraced by the royal family, his conversations with his new kin weaving the threads of a future once unimaginable.

Jane, who shared childhood memories with Sun Yi, rejoiced in their reunion. Together, they reminisced late into the night, recounting school days and the fateful rescue that had brought Sun Yi to Saipon's shores. The tale of her desperate swim, her fading strength, and the sailor's daring leap into the sea to save her was a testament to the indomitable spirit of survival.

The visit to Saipon marked a turning point for the visitors. Offered a place in this foreign land, they instead chose to return to their village, driven by a sense of duty to their roots. Prince Balzer, inspired by their commitment, vowed to support their village, transforming it into a haven that drew visitors from across the Indian Ocean.

In the fullness of time, Jane's path led her to love, marrying a brother of Sun Yi's husband in a joyous celebration in Bongboi. Moved by her journey, Jane captured the essence of her experiences in a poem, a lyrical reflection of the odyssey that had changed their lives:

Serendipity

In dance where tides and time entwine,
A message crossed the vast, blue brine.
  From prince to fisher's lucky find,
  Hope and destiny were aligned.

Amidst the ocean's autumn roar,
Hearts blend on Saipon's gentle shore.
  A daughter lost, now found once more,
  In family where love's in store.

A kingdom gave a warm embrace,
As tears of joy adorned each face.
  A sailor's leap, a saving grace,
  United paths in life's wild chase.

From humble roots to palace grand,
A trip marked by fate's unseen hand.
  A village changed by royal band,
  And love's new flair, on foreign land.

In whispers soft, fate gently sways,
A chance encounter lights the days,
  Through life's vast, unseen tapestry,
  Unfolds sweet serendipity.

Upon returning to their ancestral village, Sung was hailed by his fellow villagers. They admired his generosity and humility, even in his newfound celebrity and good fortune. "He has made life better for everyone in this village, and we are grateful for it," said one of Sung's friends while tending to a garden.

One day, at dawn, Sung made his way to the shores of the Indian Ocean and laid a wreath in the water in honor of his wife and daughter, lost to the tsunami. He settled onto a weathered bench, watching the waves carry the wreath away, lost in profound contemplation over the stark contrasts of his existence. The very ocean that bestowed his village with the daily bounty of the sea also harbored a merciless wrath, manifesting in tsunamis and calamities. Though it had claimed cherished members of his family, the ocean had also delivered him a beacon of hope—a message in a bottle that transformed his sorrow into a journey of healing. The ache for his beloved lost ones would forever linger, yet he embraced his newfound path with a heart brimming with gratitude.

As the sun climbed higher, casting a golden glow over the horizon, Sung reflected on the lessons of resilience and the power of community. He realized that his story was not just one of personal triumph but a testament to the enduring spirit of his village. Together, they had rebuilt their lives, stronger and more united than ever. Sung's journey had come full circle, and as he gazed into the vast expanse of the ocean, he knew that the legacy of love and perseverance he carried would ripple through generations to come.

16

Wings of Change

Back in 2012, nestled on the outskirts of Cottonwood Falls in Kansas, Suzie Beckton, a thirty-five-year-old divorcee, resided on a serene ten-acre estate. The property was not just a piece of land; it was a masterpiece painted by nature's own hand. The majestic fountain to the east was like the estate's beating heart, its rhythmic splashes a soothing melody that resonated throughout the grounds. To the west, the towering pines and cedars stood as stoic guardians, their evergreen boughs whispering secrets of the ancient land.

The property was a kaleidoscope of vibrant colors, with wildflowers dotting the expansive meadows like jewels. A small, crystal-clear brook meandered through, its gentle babble accompanying the chorus of birdsong that filled the air. The wildlife, from the graceful deer to the playful rabbits, frolicked in the meadows and found refuge in the cool shade of the trees.

As the seasons changed, so did the estate's character. Spring brought a burst of life, with blossoms unfurling and the scent of fresh growth in the air. Summer saw the full glory of the sun, dappling the ground through the leafy canopy. Autumn adorned the estate in a cloak of reds, oranges, and yellows, a fiery display of nature's artistry. And in winter, a serene blanket of snow transformed it into a tranquil, white paradise.

This haven, inherited from her father, was Suzie's sanctuary—a place where she could breathe, heal, and be at peace with the memories of the past and the promise of the future. It was here that she found solace in the solitude and strength in the steadfastness of the land. The beauty of the property was a constant reminder that even after the darkest storms, the earth has a way of healing itself, just as she did.

Suzie, a tall woman graced with an understated beauty, had always been destined for greatness. Her high school peers and teachers saw in her a bright future, her innate ability to uplift others making her a beacon of warmth and kindness. "She'll give you all she has, even if it leaves her with nothing," a friend once said, a testament to Suzie's selfless nature. She was admired for her equanimity, both in school and later in her career as a nurse.

Suzie's husband, Willie Nimis, was not just her high school sweetheart but the man she wholeheartedly believed was her destined soulmate. Together, they embodied the quintessential couple: he, a sharp-witted lawyer, and she, a nurse with a heart of gold. Their marriage blossomed early on, brimming with wanderlust and shared aspirations of nurturing a family. Yet, as the fourth year of their union unfurled, so did the unraveling of their once unshakeable bond.

That fateful summer, Suzie, wearied by Willie's laments of endless work hours, planned a surprise dinner to steal him away from the clutches of his office. She arrived at his firm around 7 pm, only to witness a scene that would sear her soul: Willie, entwined with the young intern, Judy Cross, in a compromising tableau. The betrayal sliced through her heart, yet it was only the beginning of an affair that would slowly corrode the very foundation of their love.

Despite Suzie's valiant attempts to mend their fractured connection through counseling, Willie's affections had irretrievably wandered. The years that followed were marred by his escalating indifference and cruelty, culminating in a divorce that Suzie embraced with a resigned grace. She relinquished any claim to alimony or their joint possessions, her sole desire being Willie's contentment, even if it carved into her own well-being.

The aftershock of their parting dealt a crushing blow to Suzie's father, whose heart gave way under the strain, passing away in the same week Willie petitioned for divorce. This loss eclipsed the sorrow of her mother's departure a decade earlier, leaving Suzie adrift in a sea of grief, yet somehow, still afloat with an unwavering hope for brighter tomorrows.

In the wake of her divorce, Suzie retreated into solitude on her estate, her once open heart now guarded and wary of new love. Her friends, alarmed by her withdrawal, attempted to reach out, but the scars Willie left were deep. Suzie's generosity of spirit remained, but the prospect of trusting another seemed an insurmountable feat. Kathy, a lifelong confidante, lamented, "Willie's betrayal cut so deep, only divine intervention could restore her faith in love."

Each morning, Suzie would lovingly feed the birds and squirrels on her property before leaving for work. She spoke to the animals as if they were old friends, and they, in turn, responded with affection to their kindhearted caretaker. Among them was a mourning dove, a brown, spotted creature with a graceful, slender tail and a small head that particularly caught her attention. It greeted her each day with its soft cooing, a gentle reminder that seemed to nudge her towards her morning prayers, which she followed devoutly at the sound of its call. Suzie had once cared for this dove when it was injured, nursing it back to health under her deck until it could return to its nest in the trees. She named the dove Sophia.

On a typical day, the birds would gather at Suzie's residence, feast on the seeds she provided, and then depart for their nests. The squirrels would scamper back to their hideaways in the trees. However, one Saturday, after being fed, Sophia lingered, cooing and flitting about, seemingly desperate for Suzie's attention. Suzie stepped out onto the yard, and Sophia led her to its nest, where another dove, possibly a male with white and brown patches, awaited. Suzie watched as Sophia shared the seeds with her partner. Could this be a sign from her feathered friend, a nudge for Suzie to open her heart to love once more? Regardless, it was a moment that lifted Suzie's spirits, a glimmer of joy in her otherwise solitary existence.

The next Saturday began with overcast skies. After her morning prayers, Suzie fed the birds, feeling an unusual weariness that made her long for rest. But Sophia, insistent with her loud cooing, seemed to plead for Suzie's company. Not wishing to disappoint her avian companion, Suzie drove to the nest, as the area was elevated, and she lacked the energy to climb. As she parked near Sophia's nest, the rains began—a deluge that sent the animals into a frenzy. The forecast had called for rain, but not this torrential downpour. Suzie watched from the safety of her car as Sophia retreated to her nest, while the rains inundated her home and the surrounding land. Trapped by the floodwaters, Suzie's car remained unscathed, a sanctuary amidst the chaos. Other vehicles were swept away, and the siding of a nearby house was carried off by the flood. It was an extraordinary amount of rain in just three hours, yet Suzie was grateful to be alive, thanks to Sophia's early warning. In the aftermath, she spent a week cleaning up the storm's damage. Fortunately, only a part of her house was affected, and contractors swiftly repaired the harm.

A month had passed when Suzie ventured into town on a balmy Saturday afternoon. The sun cast a warm glow over the bustling park, where children's laughter mingled with the sizzle of family cookouts. Suzie found a spot to park along the main street, lined with quaint shops and inviting eateries. Out of the blue, Sophia, her feathered confidant, alighted on Suzie's shoulder. Startled, Suzie queried with feigned indifference, "Sophia, what brings you here?" The dove seemed to nod and smile, as if to reassure her, "I'm here as a friend, not a source of embarrassment." In a flutter, Sophia took to the skies, leaving a flustered Suzie to collide with an approaching gentleman, Patrice Lomond, a distinguished real estate magnate of Cottonwood Falls, his coffee staining his shirt in the encounter.

"I'm terribly sorry. It was that bird—though I'm not blaming it," Suzie stammered, offering her handkerchief in a futile attempt to dab away the spill. Patrice responded with unexpected gentleness, "No harm done. I'll have it cleaned. Are you alright?" Suzie's concern was palpable as she replied, "I'm fine, thank you. But your shirt…" Introductions were exchanged, and as they parted, Patrice found himself captivated by the memory of Suzie's striking eyes, hopeful for another meeting.

With her errands complete, Suzie returned home, Sophia's coos accompanying her journey, now vibrant and playful, a stark contrast to their usual somber tone. Suzie mused over the dove's behavior—its flood warning, the chance meeting with Patrice—and accepted these mysteries with grace.

Come Monday, it was both Sophia and her mate that roused Suzie, their coos transformed into tender serenades as they feasted on seeds. That evening, Suzie's path led her back to the main street, drawn to a fragrance boutique. Fate intervened once more as she encountered Patrice amidst the scents. "I'm sorry—" she began, only to be met with his warm smile. "No apologies necessary. Our meeting was fortuitous," he assured her. He recognized the scent of Lavender perfume on her, a fragrance cherished by his late wife. Suzie offered her condolences, and in a twist of serendipity, Patrice extended an invitation to dinner. Suzie, touched by the gesture, accepted.

Throughout the week, the lovebirds' serenades replaced the once mournful coos, infusing the property with a palpable sense of joy. It seemed as if every creature was buoyed by Suzie's blossoming connection with Patrice. Their dinner at a fine restaurant in Cottonwood Falls was a dance of shared vulnerabilities and tentative hopes. Patrice spoke of his late wife with a tender reverence, expressing a readiness to honor her memory by embracing the future. Suzie, in turn, confided her past heartaches, whispering a cautious admission that perhaps her heart was ready to explore love once more. Their laughter and smiles stitched together a quilt of new beginnings as they parted with promises of another meeting.

The following week, Suzie's conversation with her high school friend Mona was a whirlwind of excitement and teasing banter. Mona's enthusiasm about Suzie's date with the town's most eligible bachelor was infectious, and despite Suzie's protests that wealth was of no consequence, Mona playfully insisted it was a happy bonus. Their laughter rang out, a celebration of potential love, with Mona's teasing prediction of wedding bells echoing in Suzie's ears as they said their farewells.

Amidst the routine of a Wednesday workday, a call from the hospital pierced Suzie's newfound tranquility. Her ex-husband Willie, now a patient clinging to life, had requested her presence. At his bedside, Suzie listened as Willie conveyed his remorse through scribbled words of contrition. The irony of his situation was not lost on her; the man who had once betrayed her was now abandoned, a victim of his own infidelities. Suzie's response was a testament to her enduring compassion—her love for Willie had evolved, no longer the romantic flame it once was, but a steady, forgiving presence. With a prayer for his recovery, Suzie offered Willie a grace that transcended their fractured past, leaving the hospital with a heart both heavy and hopeful.

The following week, Patrice visited Suzie at her estate and was captivated by its splendor—the lush greenery, the enchanting fountain, the delightful chorus of birds. He proclaimed it a modern-day Garden of Eden. As they savored the view from the balcony, Sophia, with a gentle whisper, beckoned her winged companions. The robin and other melodious songbirds offered a serenade, enveloping them in nature's symphony. Suzie, with a tender smile, gathered seeds from the barn, and together, they shared this offering with the birds. It was a moment of joy and laughter, of tender hugs and heartfelt embraces, as Patrice became acquainted with the avian members of Suzie's family. Later, they withdrew to the warmth of the family room, their hearts light, as they lost themselves in the shared comfort of watching television.

Weeks turned into months, and the bond between Patrice and Suzie only grew stronger. Their strolls through the park were enveloped in an aura of serene intimacy, where each shared secret and burst of laughter added a stroke to the canvas of their companionship. Their hands were entwined and hearts growing closer. Patrice's annual tribute to his late wife—a bottle of Lavender perfume at her resting place—spoke volumes of his enduring love and respect, touching Suzie deeply. Their compatibility was undeniable, often evidenced by the seamless way they completed each other's thoughts.

As their love story unfolded, it caught the attention of the town's gossip columns, with paparazzi vying for snapshots of their tender moments. Yet, amidst the flash of cameras, their connection remained unshaken, rooted in genuine affection and mutual admiration.

A year later, under the golden glow of the sun and against the picturesque backdrop of Chase County Lake park's waterfalls, Patrice's proposal to

Suzie was nothing short of magical. Her joyful "yes" echoed through the park, setting in motion plans for a day they would always cherish.

Autumn painted Cottonwood Falls in hues of gold and amber as the town prepared for a wedding unlike any other. The main road to the church was adorned with festive decor, and the local merchants, many of whom were Patrice's tenants, planned to close their shops in celebration. Their affection for Patrice was evident; they revered him not just as a landlord but as a cherished member of the community. Alfred, the restaurant owner, affectionately dubbed him the "Prince" of Cottonwood Falls, while others spoke of his generosity and kindness during their times of need. The town buzzed with excitement, everyone donning their finest attire, ready to witness the union of two beloved souls.

The church service was a vision of grace and joy. Family and friends held their breath in anticipation as Patrice tenderly placed the ring on Suzie's finger, sealing their vows. The day unfolded into a cascade of celebrations, with parties and receptions hosted by the myriad of friends and organizations the couple cherished. Yet, as their limousine glided from the church to the first reception, the sight of Willie, Suzie's ex-husband, in a wheelchair by the roadside, cast a shadow over her heart. In a quiet moment before the reception, Suzie's confessions to Mona, her bridesmaid were met with a stern reminder of Willie's erstwhile heartlessness. Mona's words were a stark contrast to the day's happiness, urging Suzie to focus on the present joy rather than the specters of the past.

At the main reception, Mona delivered a poem that captured the essence of the couple's journey:

The Ballad of Two Souls

In a world spun from threads of fate,
Two hearts converged, a love innate.
    Through tests of time, their bond did grow,
    A tribute to the love they show.

May laughter echo in your life,
Through times of joy, and times of strife.
    For love's a flame that burns e'er true,
    A guiding light for both of you.

As seasons change and years will pass,
Your love's a flame that e'er would last.
    Through leaves' whispers and winter's chill,
    Your hearts as one, a love that's still.

In dance of time, with hands entwined,
A blend of souls, in love, you'll find.
    The journey long, with paths unseen,
    Yet, you'll traverse, as king and queen.

May each new dawn bring joy anew,
Your twilight snug, as lovers do.
    For in your arms, the world's amiss,
    Lost in the harbor of shared bliss.

The poem was a tribute to their love, a celebration of the new chapter
they were beginning together. After their wedding, Patrice and Suzie set
off on a honeymoon filled with discovery and bliss. Upon their return,
they shared the joyous news of expecting their first child. And through
it all, Suzie continued her tender ritual of feeding the birds, a symbol of
the enduring care that defined her spirit.

SONNETS

1. Abandonment

When in my success, many friends I found,
    Fair assurances most to me did make.
Yet, in my regress, they were quite unkind,
    And in my need, promptly my side forsake.
My kindred promised me quite faithfully,
    Swearing by the Lord and their family,
To abide ever with me steadfastly,
    Yet recant their fair pledge quite startlingly.
See how sudden, away they flee from me,
    Yet, recall I, that in their pledges said,
"We'll stand firm with you, just you wait and see,"
    But now reclining in their cozy bed.
They that will say something, yet nothing do,
Aren't worthy of my good presence to go.

2. A Divine Bequest

In it, He makes great, countless promises
    To all generations of humankind.
Nothing contestable, but certainties
    Are contents of this divine bequeathed hand.
A fountain of facts, like Trevi, famous,
    With charming expressions of love and trust.
A mountain of hope like Everest, gracious,
    To the climber seeking the peak of wit.
This gift contains compacts for all in life,
    And thereafter of peace and endless bliss,
With guidance for sure triumph over strife,
    And context for pure love and joy and peace.
This gift, no one should blindly set aside,
Must be opened, and to its guides abide.

3. Anxiety And The Soul

A stress inducing world that seems to shift,
  Beneath those tired feet, while deranged demands
Fill days of distraction and heavy lift;
  No rest or sleep, no reprieve from errands.
Each moment finds the heart beating faster
  Than a fast derailing train, while restless
Legs struggle apace with sweaty, eager,
  Nervous hands; the mind in kind is feckless.
Fight for flight and perhaps, pointless worries,
  Torment a soul in expressive distress;
Its peace hijacked by false, baseless stories
  Like a husband's caught in tryst with mistress.
Overwhelming an honest mind and soul,
Without mediation, destroys the whole.

4. Appreciation In The Mundane

Brush your teeth, set your clock—life's ticking beat,
  Check doors are locked, secure against the night.
Scan your phone, walk your home, check kids have slept,
  Close your eyes, surrender to dreams' soft tilt.
Did the toothbrush impale your boorish brain,
  Or the selfish phone rob your foolish mind?
Do these oft-repeated rituals bring rain—
  Problems, some grateful moments you can't find?
Are your knees too proud to touch the ground,
  Your heavy hands too haughty to be clasped?
And your fine lips that often whisper sound,
  Cast not a word to Him whose help you grabbed?
Take time, clasp your hands, say a word or two,
To Him, for His love, endless giving true.

5. Beguiling Her Love

Felt there wasn't a chance at her affection—
    Surely, of this land's rich elite, I'm not.
No foul charm or pliant heart concoction
    Would conjure her mind to ponder this naught.
Spoke I of distress in my stressful youth,
    Oft beguiling her of her torrent tears;
She said, "twas awful, your life's ne'er been smooth,"
    And gave me for my pain, a pile of sighs.
Then spoke I of love and sweet weight of duty;
    How my heart giv'n freely, was spurned by one.
She said, "your love is pure, full of beauty,"
    Wishing God's heav'n bequeathed her such a man.
Of such is how I, her affection gained—
No tribute on my behalf was obtained.

6. Ephemeral Love

I restrained myself that night, though I felt
    Distress, and a sinking heart soiled by pain.
In the midst of the Father's throne, I knelt,
    For His mercies that will my mind regain.
Yet, He dismissed my desperate plea and said,
    "Twas what you have asked, and so twas given.
Pout not now, cause your heart is overwhelmed
    By she, whom your oft crazed mind was craving."
He spoke of things I had oft overlooked,
    Some quite fine, yet others unbearable;
That I should lie with one not my own creed,
    Proffers a bond, fleeting and unstable.
Hence, I would defer to His plans for me,
That vows no ephemeral love I see.

7. Every New Day Is A Gift

Presented fresh, one second past midnight,
　　Free of charge, free of life's many a dread.
Like baked bread, fresh in a clear oven's sight,
　　It welcomes all to hope and be well fed.
A gorgeous gift from the Master of love,
　　Like true current flow, in a flash is gone.
Yet, man isn't judged by what's hid in his glove,
　　Through use of this gift, his mettle is shown.
Does he harness the sun, sit out the rain,
　　Blame his collapse on clouds that dart the sky?
Or does he act on bold plans from his brain,
　　Transforming a forming world, aiming high?
Squander not this gift, in spite of its heft,
Make this gift count, else your life is adrift.

8. Her Deceit

Out of the bag, it has become quite clear
　　That she had prevaricated, and lied,
When inquired I, of him and her affair;
　　Me for needs, him, her heart entwined.
Stunned by learning of her double dealings,
　　A righteous rage denied me my senses;
My reason restrained not my fierce feelings,
　　Nor answered for my offing offenses.
Mine heart, fragile, couldn't handle deception,
　　She'd pierced and crossed me, coldly and boldly.
Our new baby's stirps isn't my conception,
　　And I, not the man I once was—really.
Revenge, revenge now, but how could I?
With this poor angel, perhaps I should sigh.

9. Her Villainy?

She was quite busy availing her pouch,
    In like manner to the rich and vagrant—
In need of carnal relief or as such;
    The sweaty, stinky, or sometimes fragrant.
Their arousing, rage, and female hatred,
    With secrets of shocking acts and moments,
Are presented in her prudent day-trade,
    As she sustains some needy dependents.
Perhaps, you may revile her, you righteous,
    For debauchery, or frankly villainy,
Yet, she isn't unlike those with wedded ties,
    Availing their hallowed frames to many.
She traded with doctors and raised one too;
In judgment, might not be enough for you.

10. His Call Of Redemption

Last Sunday, found myself across His cross,
    Confessing at heart, my contrarian ways.
Staring at me, He said, "Discard your dross
    And live forgiven, the rest of your days."
How oft I'm conscience constrained in this life,
    Prancing as though His advanced days were mine;
Piling vile where once were vile and strife,
    Like my limitless trysts with lust and grime.
My mind wistful, mine eyes drowning in tears,
    Then the minister scaled the dais, ranting
On the stain of sin, and those in arrears,
    Whose painful punishment awaits—haunting.
I'm sure to prefer His admonishment,
And word of mercy on my atonement.

11. His Vanished Will To Compromise

There was such a time he was quite unseen;
　　Faced vile injustice, ridiculed, besmirched,
　　Braved oppression's pain, and cruelly abused
By those apprehensive of his lifestyle's lean.
Soon gained acceptance by most in the land;
　　Sparked a reversal of long hateful years,
　　Held large revivals without slavish fears,
Cashed in on the fair people's change of mind.
With clout, became oblivious of record;
　　Subjected old foes to his conditions,
　　　　And lost his strong will to compromise.
He who once had assistance for accord
　　On his acceptance in states and nations,
　　　　Shows arrogance that may cause his demise.

12. Honor Thy Father

Last night, I read the great book of pity,
　　And 'twas clearly writ, "Honor thy father;"
With promise of mortal longevity,
　　By the most high God, Himself the Father.
While I desire ne'er His wise laws avoid,
　　Was shocked—'twas hopeless for a lad forlorn;
What if a man by choice, pursues the road,
　　Like an Asp, parting once his babe is born?
Surely, one can't honor a man unseen,
　　And He renders to man ergo his deed.
Fear ye not, keep His wise law as written,
　　He will judge those who abandon their seed.
Honor thy father in spite of their mold;
God will repay all those fathers who fold.

13. I Should Have Made A Tape

Doubted lately, the essence of learning;
    Long nights cramming books, interrupting sleep,
    Rhyme, verse, calculus for the mind to keep,
Though mind I not pioneering teaching.
Certainly, fame reigns supreme in our lands,
    Sparking starved populace crying for more;
    Bare it all tapes, chat shows, and sports they pour,
Cashing big on those glamor-probing minds.
To fellows and experts, pittance for lives saved;
    Their crazed people's judgment of due payment,
      And fitting wage for days studying late.
This I'm convinced, morality be damned;
    Given my huge natural endowment,
      School I should have skipped, and just made a tape.

14. Life's Impediments

Marching on its own, not on their own terms,
    With its unfurling beyond their control.
Challenge it, they can, head to head like rams,
    Or accept its offers, playing their role.
Each day brings issues to test their resolve,
    Like groups striving through an obstacle course.
Its riddles needing skill and grit to solve,
    And wisdom with courage as strong resource.
It can be cruel in duels with them,
    Often bankrupting and bleeding their plans,
Yet could be fulfilling if they become
    Adept at weathering storms when it rains.
Learning to march to its beat is required,
In its arena, remains undeterred.

15. Making Life's Choices

Her hands in every facet of my life,
    From rising sun till night darken the skies.
Stray I not from them, whether joy or strife,
    By her hands, my life's excellence defines.
About the speech I preach or things to do,
    The many thoughts to think or clothes to wear.
The friends to hold, or the ones to let go,
    With whom to spend time and whose voice to hear.
Her feet show at my bedside each morning,
    Pacing and boggling my oft-dawdling mind.
Her eyes staring at my stares each evening;
    Whether I would succumb or be unkind.
Her picky attitude would always show,
She's in much control over what I know.

16. Man's Pessimism

Finding its way into humble hearts of man
    In scurrilous bid to scramble his thoughts,
Like an Ivy sprawling his brilliant brain,
    Poisons his just judgment of future paths.
Grounding his endless flow of hopefulness,
    Robbing him of strength for his countless chores,
Wills his steps, to stutter in doubtfulness
    And squander those blessings the Maker stores.
He must pray that it preys not on his mind;
    Shedding suspicions when those blessings flow,
Believing the future is ne'er unkind,
    Like Ghandi, he's blessed with a buoyant glow.
While a modest dose could keep him grounded,
Its needless excess could leave him stranded.

17. Mistress Bound

Mistress bound! Despite all this wronged wife tried,
 His brash acts were like plinks from leaky pipes.
Mistress bound! All through the cold nights, she cried;
 His jaunts messed with rest, just one of her gripes.
To quell the noise, she called the blessed fitter,
 Who showed up quite quickly to mend the leak;
Counseled and read apt excerpts from scripture,
 Yet, the din crescendoed, reaching its peak.
Plink! Plink! Plink!: this mess made her quite depressed,
 To plug the leak, she discharged a loud round.
Like a calmative, her hell was suppressed;
 He'll miss his dead mistress who'd ne'er be found.
Those partners dreaming of being mistress bound,
Should consider its loud consequent sound.

18. My Ignorance of Akin Love

I cannot fathom what was just witnessed,
 Perhaps mine eyes addled by the quaking,
 Ears muddled by tremors in their making;
Rare, aired passions of two bare frames appressed.
Should I have walked away then, or stayed put?
 Indeed, twas intrusion of my acreage,
 Quite a rarity in this day and age,
Perhaps why weak-kneed I, had gone kaput.
Yet, these bold bacchants were alike sapiens;
 Gorgeous, wasp-waisted with fine glossy skin,
  Long hair, polished nails, and enchanting eyes.
Though my mind had mistook them for aliens,
 Told it's the bold new world of love, akin;
  My heart admits its ignorance, and sighs.

19. My Lustful Arrogance

'Twas quite a run in which I had my way,
    With many of her kind, I had much sway;
Oft reached my selfish goals then ran away,
    Although they had hoped, I was there to stay.
With fussy eyes, my vile arrogance spread,
    Ditched each prior for the new shining toy.
With much disdain, their dissents oft I shrugged,
    Sad for her kind but brought me lustful joy.
Or so I thought in my self-absorbed heart,
    Heedless, my just reward was in her store,
When one I took as dear and chosen part,
    Ripped me apart, ergo, in mindless gore.
My picky eyes now blind to arrogance,
And heart in newness values her substance.

20. Orphaned Of His Spirit

There are those minds, who would e'er be unkind,
    Not of Godly fear, but of things worldly;
Orphaned of His spirit, and oft are blind,
    Grasping not His virtues; rich and heav'nly.
Of riches and pleasures, they set their mind,
    Drowning in sin, and knowing not their Lord;
The love He showed, when for their sins He died,
    They oft dismiss, spoiling the blood He shed.
Perhaps it's time for those in jeopardy,
    To take good heed of their foregone ending
And do that which proffers a remedy,
    In spite of their most sinful beginning.
Those who wouldn't mend, ensure a date with hell,
Where the devil will gladly toll their bell.

21. Prayer For a Cleansed Heart

See how barren and sad she has become,
    For going against the Lord and stealing
From him, who trusted her and kept her warm,
    When her clouds were dark with shadows creeping.
Bitterly, she weeps with tears on her cheeks,
    Yet none of her kin near to comfort her.
Those who pursue her, leave her in distress;
    All her friends and kin have since betrayed her.
The Lord brought her grief for her many sins,
    Those who once honored her, now despise her,
For they saw her naked; she herself groans,
    In her deeds, had not considered the future.
She may need to seek a path with head bowed,
Hands clasped, praying to Him for a heart cleansed.

22. Sacred Error

Their guilt for the Savior's death, you assigned,
    Short of human desire to wear their shoes.
The pain for which the precious Savior died,
    You painfully imposed upon the Jews.
Amiss, you tagged them scoffers, foes of God,
    Though the good book slams degrading of man.
In blind vengeance, oft shed their blameless blood;
    With the cross, pierced crossly a threatened clan.
'Tis no mystery they have yet to succumb,
    Like Mystras once to its vile pillagers.
Like you, they've been or have now become
    God's own, in spite of impious pharaohs.
His cross was a crowning moment for all,
And must ne'er be used to defend your gall.

23. See The World Through Children's Eyes

See the worried world through the eyes of these,
    Guileless and flawless and full of promise;
With fine dreams much taller than tall pine trees,
    If snubbed, man will pine he was so remiss.
They see no color, rank, or class except
    When taught by prejudiced parents they should.
E'en so, most ignore their elders' deceit;
    Making right choices as oft as they could.
Showing concern for earth's feeble climate,
    With zeal, abhor racial rancor and grudge,
Cheer for each other, whether black or white,
    And tough choices man eschews, they don't dodge.
Man would be wise to learn from these guileless,
That in future, his deeds would be flawless.

24. Sin Of Bondage

Cursed are you in every facet of life,
    The worst of the cursed are no worse than you.
Debasing and depriving with you are rife,
    Nature yet strong to be worsted by you.
Rearing beings like herding packs of wild swine,
    Dispersing them in fields for fiscal gain.
Your whips exposing flesh in fearsome line,
    Nature yet steered their will to suffer pain.
Soiling female chasteness to sack her soul,
    Yet shockingly, her resolve wasn't chastened.
By slighting male spirit, his dreams you stole,
    But he turned stronger while your vile hand waned.
Your sin left a scab on many a soul,
Wisely, man must inter you in a hole.

25. Snatched

Beyond the boisterous media barrage,
    The awaited validation was released.
Certainly not of my mother's lineage;
    Ask her why, but I cannot—she's deceased.
Doubts were ne'er on those minds of her kindred;
    Quite fondly gave of her time and vigor,
As would a doting mother or steward
    To me, and others in this close culture.
'Tis hard to think residing in one mind;
    To hurt and to nurture of the same will.
To raise like an angel, yet being unkind;
    Mother to another in errant zeal.
That I had been snatched by she who raised me
From she who suffered, brings no joy to me.

26. The Empty Pot

He is as in a field, an empty pot,
    Stuck in obscurity amongst green grass,
Perhaps waiting its material to rot,
    Or for all things consequential to pass.
Only the wind swept pebbles and dead wood
    Pinging quite wittingly its stubborn walls,
Reveal its presence and long lasting feud
    With the world it blames—where its progress stalls.
Looking skyward for water fresh from rains,
    Though nearby flows a clear and steady stream,
And wishes respite from the sun's bright rays,
    Though nearby, shading trees are not a dream.
His senseless grudge and galling progress show,
A self-crushing stance with no will to go.

27. The Day Of The Earth

It is day for an end to division
   And for mankind to be of one sound mind;
Constant flow of spirit and compassion
   Bringing relief to a brave world, once bound.
No soul's actions soiled with self-ambition,
   Total halt to those thoughts with ill-conceit.
Shared ideals in virtue and affection,
   With selfish souls retreating in defeat.
It is the day He has long expected
   Of mankind; love, mind, and spirit the same.
Sing His praise, the devil is dejected,
   Souls will no more indulge in sin and shame.
It is the day this earth comes together;
One in love, mind, and spirit forever.

28. The Foolish Maiden

As chaste as a young nun in a nunnery,
   Purer than fresh white snow on a mountain,
And blessed with oil lamp that burned brightly,
   Each soul was eager for her to attain.
From afar emerged a tall dark figure;
   The devil who'd put the crown on evil,
Void of essence, affluent in allure,
   Who swiftly swindled her most treasured oil.
Her virtue gone, and dull as a convent,
   She'd swapped maiden oil for handsome darkness;
Yet faults all else, though in on his intent,
   Wishing she'd been much wiser in weakness.
Maidens, be sure to distance the devil;
Cede not precariously your precious oil.

29. The Good Lie

I was conceived on a gorgeous island,
   Where the flaming sun hugs fragrant flowers;
Rays sparkling on granules of golden sand,
   And palpating the emerald-blue waters.
At my mom's proud telling and retelling,
   A pretending dad, concurring, would nod
On that splendid moment for their rearing,
   That which God, the Maker, bequeathed their sod.
With honest heart, a life's past is shielded;
   Daddy's been giving to me through the years
With much love, yet his bloodline ne'er bequeathed—
   This fact kept from me in their private tears.
Their dear son's happiness first and foremost;
One secret of the past will be their inmost.

30. The Mind Keeps The Whole Intact

Hands and feet project proudly on this frame,
   Eyes and ears marking well their every move,
Yet, these soldiers joined, haven't nearly the same
   Power as him who commands their precise rove.
Though furnished with much sway, he's oft betrayed,
   By his trumpeter's frequent thoughtless talk,
Like betrothing the maiden of charade,
   Who deftly diverted this trooper's walk.
But is the chatty trumpeter to blame
   For voicing amiss that which he ponders?
Surely not; short of his consent, no claim
   Can be made, and not one soldier wanders.
Soldiers on this frame will only react.
It's that which thinks that keeps the whole intact.

31. The Rock And The Wind

His lasting love found me, lost and forlorn,
 With mercy, He embraced me as His own.
Stressing not on my sins, those days were gone,
 And true love He gave me—one I've ne'er known.
She promised me love while I was forlorn,
 Kept me in the dark about her specious plans;
In pain and much anguish, my heart did mourn,
 Pouring pain on pain like sad, purple rains.
Would I be wrong to trust Him more than her?
 Would He not see me through the purple sea?
With Him, my ship sails through storms or winds fair,
 I can but judge that which was shown to me.
He has ne'er failed; sure as ticks of the clock,
Man's love like the wind, His is like a rock.

32. Their Light Went Out

The world is full of places where the lumens
 Are low, or perhaps permanently out;
Its power ceased by powers, or crazed men's
 Might, through arrogance and perilous fight.
With dreadful aura, sad and depressed,
 By the doom and gloom permeating the air,
Its days and nights alike are night possessed,
 With drunk dragons dominating its sphere.
Nothing picturesque, and nothing dreamy,
 But thugs amputating human spirits,
With disfigured victims' pleas for mercy
 Ignored in their hardly disguised units.
E'er stay you in such grand places stated,
Pray your life's joys stay illuminated.

33. Tussle With Sin

Like a beauteous queen enchanting the eyes,
    You torment the pure hearts and souls of man;
With luscious, sinister charms which outsize
    Your righteous sister's, oft the also-ran.
Your thrill and enchantment are oft deceit,
    On my weak mind, allured by deeds of ease,
While vile, brief pleasures convey much conceit
    To minds with self-desires that would not cease.
Stuck with tortured trails of pain and regret,
    With anxious glimpses of darkness and death,
I will prolong no more this vile abet
    Of your fraud and conceit, in length and breadth.
You are vile and wrong for me, this I'm sure,
And have wronged those captured in your rapture.

34. Remedy Of Disappointment

Enough! You've made life unusual and rough,
    From early nonage years past puberty,
Reveling oft in constant, cold rebuff,
    Dashing hopes and mocking my sanity.
Like a bride deserted at the altar,
    You've proffered profound pain to this pure heart;
Distressing, gut-wrenching—branding your scar
    On mind once cheerful with chances to chart.
Depart from me with your pompous pals too;
    Tension, depression, seclusion, and shame.
In time, my once sweet spirit will renew,
    And will upset your upsetting of me.
My trust, still intact, will guide my tread,
In my chances to thrive and make my bread.

35. Winter's Cold

Winter's cold has chilled your charming presence;
    With merry bells muffled by mournful knell,
Boughs of holly shamed by lilies' essence,
    And solemn songs drown joys your carols tell.
But for you, winter's void of jolly sense,
    Fraying those frozen hearts your tinsels cheer.
Yet, in twain, ushered sorrows quite intense;
    Through loss and anguish, filial ties did tear.
Unlike the e'er merry Hallmark satires,
    Your joy, oft grinning in this heart of mine,
Frowns lately; its cheery essence retires,
    As in last winter's end of mom's bright shine.
Enough! Bring back those choirs and merry bells,
With hope and joy and peace, their chorus swells.

36. World's Maiming Toys

Flew I, a merry bird, around the world,
    In much surprise, saw what wasn't there before;
Zones with marked edges, at sea or on land,
    And white-suited men on grey ships ashore.
At length, saw I fences guarded by corps,
    And men in white coats proofing maiming toys.
The ingress gates shut, their signs writ with words,
    "Restricted…;" once places of countless joys.
So head I north—a quite familiar zone,
    Bulging from earth were lethal, larger toys,
Long and slender, could touch many a zone,
    Binding my joys, and this my hope destroys.
Certainly, those lethal toys aren't for kids.
In zonal tensions, they're just opening bids.

OTHER POEMS

1.   A Bowl Of Dust And Ashes

Strolled in my garden that day;
    Yellow daffodils were scorched,
Yet not from the sun's array.
    Lean lilies in black were clad,
Cup-less tulips like friars
    With hands raised, giving last rites,
A bowl of dust and ashes,
    Where once a fountain with lights.
Asked I, of the dove perplexed,
    On the din and disorder,
She said, "Surprised you were spared,
    'Tis man's moral disaster."

2.   A Bright Future

1.   There is no guarantee,
    Life will be trouble-free,
'Tis sure some setbacks one shall see
    Are vast as open sea.

2.   Oft one's many defeats
    Are vanishing mishaps,
For new days bring hopeful drumbeats,
    That drown those sullen harps.

3. Tomorrow's tasks to face,
    With hope and confidence.
All bitter reflections erase,
    In spite of turbulence.

4. The sun will ever rise,
    Amidst those cloudy days.
The faithful ones see no demise,
    In their bright shining rays.

3. A Dying Love from Both Sides

1. A thriving love is full of fun,
Its dying rife with vengeance, oft
On faultless offspring spun as pawn,
Banned from nonage normalcy, yet
Proud he was formed by both sides.

2. Bearing the sheer terror of being
At courtside of custodial fight;
Grownups failing to grasp the sting
Of splitting on a frail lad's plight.
His needs blind-eyed by both sides.

3. Storing the stain of its collapse,
Resentment from its suitors' scorn;
'Tis screams, sarcasms, snubs, and snaps,
Echoes of fights from night till morn,
He oft endured from both sides.

4. Shamming the shame of sharing hate
    And rage retained from futile tryst;
    The proxy abuse in full spate
    Like odious blows without a mitt,
    His body braved from both sides.

5. In pain and sorrow, oft, he ploughed,
    Through tracks of neglect and of doom;
    With fading dreams, poor, sore head bowed
    And frantic cries in amber gloom,
    His pleas deaf-eared by both sides.

6. Hate, he holds not against the pair,
    In spite of raw, misplaced rage, yet
    Hopes this besets no love affair,
    And prays frail, guileless lads will get
    Nothing but love from both sides.

4. A New Perspective Unveiled

1. Two was too perfect for his life,
        For they would tear and criticize
    The motes of friends and foes alike,
        And warp his will to compromise.

2. He would his counterparts inspect
        Like probing doctors at their best,
    Scanning their beauty, and dissect
        Their moves, intent, and humble nest.

3. Reduced to one—one half of whole,
        His perceived flaws of friends removed.
    Like magic, he had grown a soul,
        Which those oft slighted friends embraced.

4. He mingled with his counterparts,
   Gracefully felt their warm embrace,
   And smelled their roses, heard their hearts,
   Beat just as his, with loving trace.

5. Often it takes adversity
   To see more than with captious stare.
   Let not a sensory scarcity
   Be your motivation to care.

5. Always Be Grateful

1. With sordid times and horrid days,
   How can I be cheerful?
   Yet, I'm reminded in my ways
   To always be grateful.

2. A gift to us and counterparts,
   With words from lips graceful,
   And smiling faces, humble hearts,
   Relaxing, and joyful.

3. Think of the oft ill-tempered beast,
   Or scoundrel quite hateful.
   Though oft they seem to have a feast,
   Their hearts are disdainful.

4. Whene'er you think about your life,
       Surely, remain grateful,
   For the future could bring new strife;
       Distasteful and mournful.

5. Good, grateful souls receive favors
       Than those who are woeful;
   For they care not on their labors,
       But often stay joyful.

6.   America's Abuse

1. Of late, she has endured abuse,
   From those who perpetrate their ruse
       To dominate her mind;
   They rage against her poor and weak,
   Stoke strife, division in their streak,
       To make her quite unkind.

2. They deny facts and proofs they see,
   Her tenets of democracy,
       Aping a vile despot;
   Loathe her fine multi-cultured grace,
   Disdain and rail against the race,
       Of some in her vast pot.

3. Their use of terror to achieve,
   Those ends which ballots cannot give,
       Chagrins her faithful throng;
   In silly rage, her lawmen beat,
   Breached her chaste democracy's seat,
       And reveled in their wrong.

4. But sadder yet are those who have
   Pledged their allegiance, her to serve,
      But steer against their oath;
   They peddle in conspiracy,
   That's counter to their literacy,
      Which is stunting her growth.

5. They brought shame to her once proud name,
   Of tyranny, have fanned the flame,
      Eager, her house to burn;
   But she is wise and resilient,
   For God blessed her with discernment,
      That will this evil spurn.

7. Anchored In Belief

1. Often sorely in pain, I asked,
      "Where is my confidence?"
   With no response, I oft remained
      In my lone residence.

2. With doubts and fears twice multiplied
      In every incident,
   I searched for clues that can't be reached;
      This was no accident.

3. I failed to acknowledge my fears,
      Knowing the consequence,
   Of little faith in Him that hears,
      My prayers with confidence.

4. No longer does my heart demand,
    "Where is my confidence?"
No longer does my heart demand,
    Through His inheritance.

5. His everlasting love is true,
    In its full providence,
Confirming that His way is sure,
    By His omnipotence.

8. Appreciation Prayer

1. Make us acknowledge the present,
    Dwelling ne'er on the past,
Help us focus on our blessings,
    So our sorrows won't last.

2. Grant us wisdom to be thankful,
    For those gifts that we have.
Shedding bitterness and envy,
    For those we do not have.

3. Help us accept whate'er has been,
    And for them, be thankful.
Grant us faith for your great promise;
    Eternally joyful.

4. May we always seek compromise,
    In our disagreement,
Grant us the will to sheath the sword,
    Using moral judgment.

9. Asked Him To Lend A Hand

Asked Him to lend a hand,
The Father kept His word,
And in my quiv'ring hand,
Was silver and pure gold.
Asked I love of mankind,
They grabbed my gold and fled,
While I confounded stood,
At morn, armed, they appeared
For my silver—quite bold.
The Father to them said,
"Ask yours, return his gold,
Before I strike you dead."

10. Balancing Acts In Love

1. My life has seen much compromise,
        They claimed won't work for me.
    Its gist they fail to recognize,
        Only weakness they see.

2. They stressed the times in vain I tried
        In my relationships;
    That I was oft eager to yield
        In lopsided courtships.

3. They failed to cite the many crops,
        My oft concessions yield,
    Like times I stopped massive teardrops,
        From drowning hearts besieged.

4. They cite other relationships,
   Where one spouse gets his way,
As good model for my courtships
   In which I'll have much sway.

5. They failed to see accords, just dread
   Like times love's spouse is brash;
Yet sometimes, one wins household bread,
   While one, takes out the trash.

6. Each life is full of compromise,
   As much a heart can do.
I'll always seek to compromise,
   And pray partners do too.

11. Beneath Her Elm Tree

1. The sun emerged, leaves came alive,
   Up from yesterday's endless work,
   Enriching fields for all to thrive,
   Survive, without being burden stuck.
   Twas life under her elm tree.

2. Summer sees leaves with sprawling hands
   Ensure respite, supplies abound;
   Viands from rain, shelter from shades,
   For buds, branches, and guests aboard.
   Gratuities of her elm tree.

3. Through vicious storms, dear leaves protect
   Her anxious residents from dread;
   Headwinds and fierce barrage reject,
   Yet, cease not making humble bread,
   Unyielding on her elm tree.

4. Mild autumn winds bring joyous smiles,
   On prancing leaves with colors bright,
   Grateful for sageness, not for miles,
   Knowing soon Christmas is fortnight,
   With bright lights on her elm tree.

5. Harsh winters on her leaves have called,
   Nurture's pearls to nature succumb.
   Long its presence was presupposed,
   Shielding, raising with like aplomb
   All those beneath her elm tree.

6. Through much dexterity displayed,
   With sacrifice, her brood sustained.
   In sooth, some tears, yet not dismayed;
   Four score and eight years, dearly yearned
   By all beneath her elm tree.

12. Beneath His Wings

1. A restful heart, a restful sleep,
       Protection full and free.
   In shadow of His wings, He'll keep
       Me safe, from what may be.

2. In this realm with many a fight,
       Confusing and contrived,
   His armor keeps me quite upright,
       Through terror, cold, and mad.

3. In secret places He shall hide
       Me from the devil's snare.
   No scheming from the evil side
       Shall e'er my living scare.

4. Trusting in Him, I ever will,
    To guard me from grave harm.
  In dicey moments, trust Him still,
    He will restore the calm.

13. Beside And Beyond

1. She asked nothing of me but love,
    And love I furnished in bundles;
  The precious moments and the trove
    Of memories bright as lit candles.

2. I asked the same of her and more,
    And she displayed her kinder side,
  By giving all she'd kept in store,
    Picking me up, and stayed beside.

3. Mornings are brighter, nights are days,
    My steps don't stutter, dreams are clear,
  When she is near and gently says,
    "Till death, I'll love you yet, my dear."

4. There's nothing more to ask of her,
    For she is just what this life needs.
  The best of dames both near and far
    Are no match for her distinct deeds.

5. The best of her, I often see;
    She lives to love and gives to live.
  The best of my lifetime will be,
    Ever with her, my love to give.

14. Beyond The Grasp Of Yesterday

1. Sometimes we must accept the man
        On his own terms, not as we want.
    Oft he tries to constrain the mind;
        Will ne'er relent but wrest and taunt.

2. No bitterness or angst can change,
        His record keeping on our lives,
    Tears and regret would only make
        Him gain a stronghold on our vibes.

3. Neither will those many complaints,
        Which feed into his selfish vaunt.
    His hurts and emotional strains,
        Sap our longed eagerness to count.

4. One's contempt to forgive, forget
        Is confirmation of his sway.
    A backward vision is consent,
        For him to meddle, overstay.

5. He is as much as advertised,
        Wise it would be to learn from him.
    Yet ne'er the urge with him abide,
        Else, ever will be on his whim.

6. 'Tis pointless to reopen wounds
        Through self-destructing exercise,
    When clearly our future portends,
        Blessings for us to realize.

15. Charity's Curse

'Tis harder being charitable,
  Far more effortless being selfish;
Though oft man is much capable,
  Taking's more facile than to fish.
Takers presume, and demand more,
  Shockingly, oft in mocking rude,
Think distraught donors of their store;
  Why bear this cross, mankind is crude?
In their ill-will, folks will inquire
  On a gen'rous gent's well intent,
And this madness dents his desire;
  His cent is better kept than spent.

16. Clothed by His Grace

1. Pestered by the primal burden,
      Suffered in Satan's tryst.
    Naked from the sins of Eden,
      Clothed by the grace of Christ.

2. At the cross, I stand forgiven,
      Its shadow shading me,
    From dangers, foes, and derision,
      Which oft my sad eyes see.

3. The Lord guides sinners to heaven,
      Yet they must be immune,
    Against those powers that threaten,
      Their plan for God's commune.

4. To Him all praise and glory giv'n,
        The Son of the most high,
    With the saints in heaven has ris'n,
        And to each heart is nigh.

17. Conscience Of Mercy

1. Turning the cheek is grand lesson
        On man's maturity.
    Seventy-seven times seven,
        Hasn't ambiguity.

2. Quicker to anger, swift to blame,
        Is his ability.
    Slower yet to forget, his shame
        And inadequacy.

3. Too hard to realize, he cries,
        In weak fragility,
    Yet hopes one he's aggrieved, regards
        It on his crudity.

4. Much power it avails to man,
        And peace infinitely,
    When he rejects the urge to ban
        His conscience of mercy.

18. Crimson Echoes

1. My blood was spilled the other night,
   A razor went awry,
   It flawed my face; an awful sight,
   Causing my heart to cry.

2. My panic made it all the worse,
   When poor recourse I tried,
   I shouted, "this must be a curse,"
   As if my spirit died.

3. Each drop I shed, stained my scarred face,
   Like sins my life impaled;
   Its deluge caused my heart to race,
   My mind was overwhelmed.

4. In echo, thought of nothing else,
   But how our Lord suffered,
   With stabs and gashes; cuts from pelts,
   Pain from being crucified.

5. Yet not a pout or curse was heard,
   In all that He endured,
   His wounds, not one with error clad,
   But by the Maker planned.

6. Each crimson drop, man's sins erased,
   To hell, no more is bound.
   Each breath He spent, new life regained,
   By blest saints in His fold.

19. Dead Was I

1. Dead was I in my devices
    And desires of my heart;
    Emptiness from earthly sources,
    Lingered in things I sought.

2. Houses, lovers, vintage autos;
    New toys in each my store.
    Yet my life drifted apropos,
    Away from heaven's shore.

3. Dead in spirit, dead in thinking,
    Dead in God's charity.
    Dead in merit, dead in living,
    Dead; my heart's purity.

4. Now in Christ my heart rejoices,
    Living water, He gives.
    With a kind mind and right choices,
    I thank my God, He lives!

20. Deceivers' Masquerade

Angel swains granted hidden horns,
    Their three trips; I, bewitched,
By songs of love with lips of thorns,
    Succumbed their bait and switch.
The first blew kisses at my heart
    With a blade in my back,

The next, nice flowers in her pot,
    Crushed my bones in her pack,
The last with specious voices said,
    "I love you, be with me,"
"Surely," said I, "accede accord
    Of fairness;" off fled she.

21. Divine Ironies

1. My God has never let me down,
Save for the time, He let me down
    My plane, spiraling in the air,
    Full of vices, and things unfair.

2. My God has never put me out,
Except the time, He put me out
    Connubial house, which was afire,
    Through my self-destructing desire.

3. My God has never shut me out,
Save for the time, He shut me out
    Those rooms, He knew weren't good for me,
    That dread and grief, my eyes won't see.

4. My God has never turned away,
Except the times, He turned away
    To let me wander, blind and lost,
    Til I sought Him with humble heart.

22. Divine Providence

1. His joy to earth endowed,
      His peace He oft provides,
   Abundantly, without a charge,
      To folks of all divides.

2. Tonight when you retire,
      You must have no desire
   To doubt any His promises,
      But to His love aspire.

3. His abundance is more
      Of spirit than of things.
   Yet, all of your wide-ranging needs,
      Eternally He brings.

4. So, claim His joy and peace,
      And spirit for your keep,
   For much abundance He has poured,
      As shepherd to a sheep.

23. Dreams In Action

1. I used to dream of finer things,
      Trusted they will come true,
   Like many hopeful human beings,
      My fulfilment was few.

2. Each new dream brought motivation
      To seek my heart's desire.
   So, I put dreams into action,
      Hoping things will catch fire.

3. My fulfilment was much sweeter
        Than what those dreams had said;
    My daring actions scaled greater
        Than feathered dreams combined.

4. There's place for dreams in every mind,
        Where hope and faith abound,
    'Tis a force that restive minds find
        To breach each mighty bound.

24. Echoes Of Doubt

1. He oft constrains my mind in bout
        That never seems to cease,
    And each time, he wins out in rout,
        With confidence and ease.

2. He makes me question future plans,
        My own abilities,
    And stranger yet, the divine hands
        With immense qualities.

3. He nudges, double-check the mind
        For outcomes quite routine,
    To check the motives of mankind,
        Their every move to screen.

4. "Defer what can be done today,"
        Is oft his great advice,
    Then rewards me from day to day,
        With restless nights, my prize.

5. His pugilistic instinct stirs,
       Whene'er my faith resumes,
    And overbearing spirit bars
       That which my hope consumes.

25. Echoes Of Envy

1. Their harsh whispers, I always hear,
    And rash judgments they sometimes air,
    About my life and kind of way,
    Of which they have a lot to say;
    My couches clean, not inherent they presume,
    And my progress, their eyes perceive, they consume.

2. Their sad chatter, oft in the dark,
    And petty grudge that light their spark,
    About my life and kind of way,
    Which they know less about to say;
    He was his mum's best, and this they much detest,
    Yet clueless, her fatuous acts my life beset.

3. Sometimes they draw quite close to me,
    Not on my cares, but things they see
    That boost my life and kind of way,
    Spiteful about, yet want a say;
    Too large a house, nicer cars, and lovely spouse,
    Yet grasp not the grouse that wedded ties arouse.

'Tis sad to see their hearts in vain,
*   In need, yet would never exceed*
The envy, which their lives constrain;
*   Perhaps this plague they'll ban indeed,*
And their hearts will delight attain.

4. Should ne'er focus on what I've got,
    But seek instead to stand apart,
    Not like my life, and kind of way,
    But won't! On me, they crave a say;
    Then, perhaps wear my shoes, what have they to lose?
    But won't! Cause abuse and ruse are tools they use.

26. Eden's Redo

"God is God," she told the serpent,
Satan stumped, selects atonement,
    Tree of knowledge yet intact.
Jesus stays with God in heaven,
Adam's roaming Eden's garden,
    Angels watching heaven's tract.
Wars and famine, nonexistent,
Floods and earthquakes, not persistent,
    Earth sees not the Father's wrath.
Death is dead! And never meets us,
Toils and sickness never sees us,
    Good from evil; no impact.

27. Equal In Dust

1. As I walked past the place of rest,
   My mind in awe was stirred.
   While wants and worries stress, and pest,
   Should they, indeed? I mused.

2. The dirt impartial to the frame,
   Of man or flow'r, the same;
   One with the soil entwined became,
   The other, blooms of flame.

3. The marble stones of each are writ,
   With addresses correct,
   Yet tenants claim not the receipt,
   Of any flowers sent.

4. No doors or locks, no space for cars,
   To nature, under stars.
   Yet absent here, the strife and scars,
   That oft one bears and hears.

5. 'Tis clear that one should never hold,
   So dear, those worldly wealth.
   At rest, within earth's gentle fold,
   None can claim wealth in depth.

28. Eternal Gratitude

1.   We thank Thee, Lord, for lives well spent,
      Who from this earthly realm retire,
  Yet with their Savior's full consent,
      In heav'n appear.

2.   Free from life's sorrow, grief, and pain,
      New strength and heartiness their gain,
  Yet in their Savior's love remain,
      In His full reign.

3.   Gone are their tears from mortal years,
      Released from conflicts, cares, and toil,
  The Lord ensures there are no fears,
      On heaven's soil.

4.   And from their labors, promised rest,
      Upon the Savior's humble breast,
  With blessings poured at His behest,
      Their lives at best.

5.   And with their rest, they serve Him still,
      For gentler, richer is that life;
  Where saints unhindered do His will,
      Is free of strife.

6.   Not as their days of toil and care,
      Their weary mortal hours sufficed,
  Yet with their spirits primed to share,
      Thy love, O Christ!

29. Façade Of Fidelity

1. Theirs seemed a love of endless bliss,
     Where much affection reigned,
   And neighbors' eyes would roll whene'er
     Public fondness they showed.

2. Disaster struck just as the pair
     Marked one score years espoused,
   His lovely wife was bound in bed
     And to illness succumbed.

3. Soon he would wed a nearby dame,
     Loathed by his deceased wife,
   And neighbors scratched their heads in shock
     At this turn in his life.

4. But long before his wife's passing,
     Displayed duplicity,
   With the same dame now his dear wife
     In awful perfidy.

5. To others, it was no secret
     Of his adulterous trysts,
   So too his now departed wife,
     Who forgave his deceits.

30. Facets Of Her Essence

'Tis often said by man,
There are two sides to a lady;
The one that loves her man,
The other makes him squirm.
But no offense, my love,
There is more than two, my baby,
Three of which I am sure,
And others in your core.
The third is quite complex;
For things which often are shady,
No man's brain can compare
With wit of women, rare.

31. Faith's Solitary Path

Expect not a faith journey
With timorous Christians,
Cause you are on your own.
Dreams of peace and normalcy,
In spite of life's burdens,
You'll carry as your own.

They'll read the Book as story
With you in faith lessons,
Yet trust in God—your own.
Pressing for love, amity,
Amidst tribal tensions,
You'll attain all alone.

Hoping for world of treaty,
Amidst warring factions,
You'll bear this cross alone.
Sad to say, but I'm sorry
That timorous Christians,
Oft abandon their own.

32. Family Gossiper

1. In love and notions, quite naïve,
      In spite of age and bent;
   For her sad gossips often have
      A self-harming effect.

2. She yaps with kin, cunning and proud,
      With hidden ax to grind;
   With laughter and applause they prod,
      For more vice from her mind.

3. They make her feel she's wonderful,
      The more her talk is rife,
   With things slanderous and spiteful,
      Causing others much strife.

4. In time, she has not well erase,
      Her mind from malice ties,
   Her sycophants heap silly praise,
      Which nourishes her vice.

5. She's not aware, her kin dishes,
      On things that she has said;
   Disdain of others, ill-wishes,
      All to the world are bared.

33. Filial Duplicity

1. Smiling faces don frowning hearts,
    Cloaked in their conduct around me;
    'Tis pointless work judging these acts,
    Whether we are on land or sea.
    Asked I, not for alms or pity,
    'Tis their game of duplicity.

2. Lavish flattery from scornful lips,
    Like rain and sun in foggy duel;
    Ponder I oft, who pen their scripts,
    Soaked in fibs, and dark gossip fuel.
    Asked I, not for their loyalty,
    'Tis their game of hypocrisy.

3. Sad to see this shameful deceit,
    Well discharged by companions near;
    Oft my own blood, per the receipt,
    Whose hearts must treasure holy fear.
    Asked I, just their sincerity,
    Yet, their game of dishonesty.

34. Forbidden Fruit's Hold

1. Although I try to free my mind
        From her fetter on me,
    I'm much conflicted and constrained;
        This flaw, my eyes can see.

2. She makes it soft and easy, oft
        To assuage my angst,
    And offers more without a fight;
        Her gift, I'm ne'er against.

3. Her apple is quite the allure,
        Just as in Eden's past;
    Weakness, surrender will conjure,
        Surely, her hold would last.

4. Each failed attempt at resistance,
        Compounded by anew;
    The appeal of her succulence
        Shows my prospects are few.

5. Regret, my mind, each night would clash,
        Yet, wash away at day,
    When she presents the apple fresh
        In such a carnal way.

6. Hope that courage, someday I'll find
        To end my surest worst,
    For she with someone else is tied;
        For my penance, I must.

35. Fury Unleashed

Earthquakes, hurricanes,
    Sudden tempests rough,
Large blasts, deluged dams,
    Snaps and cold rebuff.
Effects of these blights,
    And those forces tough
Like Etna's magmas,
    Would ne'er be enough
To quell the furies,
    Or contest the huff
Of a woman scorned.

36. Garden Of Life

In the lovely garden of life,
Its fragile flowers well aligned;
Morning daffodils start the day
With sunshine eyes, brighten the way,
Orchids and roses binding ties
By which new generations rise,
Daisies toil in the summer sun,
Dahlias bear beauty of autumn,
Blue bells ring out the grave news bold,
"Send the cold cook with marigold."
The late, wilted lilies mourned,
In the lovely garden of life.

37. Harmony's Embrace

1. They may have just enough to care,
    Perhaps not e'en enough to share.
        Yet often, they share believing
        That giving is worth their living.

2. A heart may have once been broken
    By a suitor; quite smooth-spoken.
        Yet, this ordeal brought a new friend,
        Aiding an ailing heart to mend.

3. Their quite thriving nation was blessed
    With finest of weapons assessed,
        But never stirred conflicts perverse;
        Their disputes resolved with discourse.

4. Now imagine a world of these,
   Where each beating heart is at ease;
     Sharing and caring and loving,
     Cheering for the peace it's seeking.

38. His Likeness

God will impose judgment on those
Who gaze their eyes on sinful shows;
Deign to dumb idols, thumb their nose
At Him who shields from foes and woes.
He shows like man with eyes and nose,
Yet ne'er must man His might suppose.
Perhaps a mere mirror glimpse shows
How close is He to those He chose;
The eyes wink bright like angel glows,
The nose is quite like heaven's rose.
Man is like Him; like Him, man knows
The laws on lures of sinful shows.

39. Humans Are Not Foolproof

1. His pregnant wife in time supplied
     A new cub for their fold.
   In graceful steps, he leapt and danced;
     'Twas a sight to behold.

2. He loved and cared for his dear cub,
     And groomed like a dad would.
   Though illness did his time absorb,
     He cared as much he could.

3. On his deathbed, he kindly asked
       That all God's truth be bared,
   About the cub he'd long believed
       Belied others he had.

4. Then the truth arbiter made known,
       Scores from lineage test,
   Showing the cub, now fully grown
       Was unalike his rest.

5. In a frank chat, his wife he faced,
       Which was ineffable;
   For with straight face, his fierce wife strafed,
       Facts irrefutable.

6. While he lay dying, she prolonged
       The lie in spite of proof,
   Proving humans can't be presumed
       To ever be foolproof.

40. Hush Neath The Stones

Tread here lightly dear people,
She who dwells here is simple
At heart, yet annoyed by noise,
And vagabonds without poise.
Neath these stones, no one hollers;
No noise, but from rain showers.

41. Hymn Of Mercy

1. Savior, Thy name I praise,
   My piteous pleas I raise,
   Humbly, I come.
   Hear Thou the prayers I make;
   My pains and burdens take,
   For love and mercy's sake,
   A glad outcome.

2. In the rough seas of life,
   Their waters wrought with strife
   That overwhelm;
   May my ship safely sail
   Through horrors that assail,
   My glad heart grateful, hail
   Thee at the helm.

3. When low my spirit lay,
   Proud foes around me say,
   "Give up the fight;"
   Thy guiding angels may
   Sustain me day to day,
   And hide me in their stay
   From terror's blight.

4. By Thy passion, I see
   Love proffered full and free,
   Devotedly.
   May I spread love like Thee,
   As thine own spirit be,
   And safely dwell with Thee,
   Eternally.

42. Hymn To A Reconciling God

1. Our God is reconciling
   Through Jesus Christ, our Lord.
   Salvation is entrusting
   To man, as one with God;
   Our errors notwithstanding,
   No shame, despise, or blame.
   For God is true and loving,
   And e'er will be the same.

2. Our trespasses not counting,
   In spite of breadth and heft,
   And spirits not condemning,
   Though judgments would be just;
   Peace through the cross He's given
   To worthless mind and soul.
   New life through love has proven
   That He will save the whole.

3. Our sins no more remembered;
   In depths of seas interred.
   Forgiveness He has tendered
   To spirits once defiled;
   The pow'rs of hell shall shiver
   At sight of man with God.
   This bond shall never sever
   With Jesus Christ as Lord.

43. In Devotion's Pursuit

1. My God, Thy will, I will pursue
        In this tough earthly fight,
    In spite of all that will ensue,
        I'll flourish in Thy sight.

2. Not man, his wisdom to pursue,
        Nor his fast fading prize,
    But seek Thee for Thy guidance true,
        Unblemished, right, and wise.

3. Where'er I am, whate'er I be,
        May You be e'er with me;
    May e'er my soul be poured in Thee,
        Thy spirit flows in me.

4. My life devoted to Thy will,
        Will e'er be full and free.
    Grant Lord that I may trust Thee till
        I rest in heav'n with Thee.

44. It Lives On Heaven's Shore

1. It lives on heaven's shore
        And is its brightest star,
    Burns sinful clouds straggling its core,
        Though many miles afar.

2. It shades earth's forests green,
        Nurtures its grains of wheat,
    Restores its places floods have been;
        Like lands which rains defeat.

3. It often aids the rain,
       Return to the azure;
    Their righteous, foggy fight is gain;
       For earth, its mists assure.

4. It scorches earth with fire,
       Blazing many a path,
    For shrubs and forests to retire,
       Yet, maintained by its wrath.

5. Its anger sometimes flares,
       With tensions near a spot.
    Yet, its tug holds those heav'nly beings
       From falling far apart.

6. It travels east to west,
       With its broad smile and heat,
    Yet, on heav'n's shore, its heart is set,
       South; earth by it is blest.

45. Jeremiah's Prophecy

1. He warns nations shall be destroyed,
    Disaster all around them spread;
       Floods and tempests tear their terrain,
       Laying waste their once peaceful plain.

2. Those slain by God will ne'er be mourned,
    But strewn like litter on the ground;
       With nations trapped by God's decree,
       Their kings shall have no place to flee.

3. Fear Him, ye saints, to heed his word,
   And bow in reverence to your God;
       Depart from evil ways and schemes,
       Lest He destroy your hopes and dreams.

46. Legend Of Familial Ties

1. Traipsing oft through buoyant gladness,
   Sudden loss and solemn sadness,
   Days of love and social madness,
   Others too for moral weakness.
   These are features of familial ties.

2. Birthday wishes and mixed dishes
   Assemble in frequent meetings;
   Pleasant moods when each heart ditches
   Grudges, hurts, and past enmities.
   The festal form of familial ties.

3. Loans oft aren't entirely repaid,
   And borrowed pieces ne'er returned.
   Ask not reasons for debts delayed
   Else, hearts afire might get you burned;
   Frequent failings of familial ties.

4. Those once holding a helping hand,
   Advancing them to Eminence,
   May scorn requests of brothers bound
   By needs that may enhance their chance;
   The falsity of familial ties.

5. At times, their burdens, one may hold,
    Yet others, fruitless, get acclaim.
    In their struggles, seeks one accord
    While the rest battles to defame;
    The forlornness of familial ties.

6. Some will oft bow down in prayer
    For graces grand on a sister,
    And with their gifts and cheer appear
    At bedside of a sick brother;
    The faithfulness of familial ties.

7. In shock and sadness, gather oft,
    Yet grateful for those lost and loved.
    Sing sacred songs, somber and soft,
    With tears and cheers for lives well lived;
    The fond farewell of familial ties.

8. Like the air we breathe, its needed,
    By all seeking life's true courtship.
    E'en in clans with minds conceited,
    Lie pure hearts yearning for kinship;
    Life will e'er furnish familial ties.

47. Love's Prayer

1. May no man or woman sever,
   Us from union, strong and fair,
   And no wind of harm blow stronger
   Than the breath of love we air.

2. May we speak each other's language,
   As we grow from age to age,
   And our acts be like birds' plumage,
   Brightly streaming on love's stage.

3. May we ever keep our promise
   To be faithful, kind, and true;
   That our hearts will ne'er be remiss
   To confer each other's due.

4. May our love be e'er like sunshine,
   Cast upon those gloomy days,
   In dark nights ever the lifeline,
   That'll keep our hearts ablaze.

5. May our love flow like a river;
   Sparkling, peerless, deep, and free,
   Darting obstacles, meander,
   Till it meets its hallowed sea.

48. Love's Redemption's Promise

If we could do over again,
I would be a better man;
Not he, who caused you so much pain,
For with time, this heart did learn
That his love was selfish and vain.
I don't know what happened then,
That this heart would've so much disdain,
But he's gone; I'm a new man.

Once, you viewed me as your idol
Like in sweet dreams, oft you'd tell,
Where I'm playing well the lead role,
Saving you from dreadful spell.
Truth is, love's idols sometimes fail,
Yet, a new man, who'll give all
Is here with you, whate'er befall;
I know our love will prevail.

So darling give me a chance then
To play a lead role again,
Both in your dreams and for certain,
Bringing joys that'll drown your pain.
I will never hurt you again,
And with time your trust regain;
You and I riding our love's train
To where endless lovers reign.

49. Lust To Light

1. Lust, once you were my pleasure,
     Lurking quite oft in my mind;
    Fleshy orgies, things of leisure,
     Urging me to be unkind.

2. Lust, once my only weakness;
     Holding out for my last gasp,
    Yielding oft to sensual sweetness,
     Keeping me within your grasp.

3. Lust, once you were my treasure,
     Stocked my store with pleasures rare;
    Pretty forms with finest of hair,
     Of their morals, I didn't care.

4. Lust, once my heart was hopeless,
     Dropping old for the new frame;
    Oft perceiving not their worries,
     In my mind, twas just a game.

5. Lust, your scheming is wicked,
     Preying oft on weak men's minds;
    Like they, mine was bound and crooked,
     By your vile will to coerce.

6. Lust, enough of your tenure,
     I decline all that you give;
    My new mind will fore'er endure,
     With fair morals, I will live.

50. Mother, An Endless Treasure

1. Seen one over a wooden cot,
      Coaxing a little baby sleep?
   Or met one in a prostrate state,
      Pleading for a lad's safety keep?

2. I saw one brave the heavy rains,
      Besetting those familiar ties;
   Through daunting days and haunting pains,
      Stayed quite resilient, true, and wise.

3. We've seen those bitter, copious tears,
      Shed by those doting, wistful eyes,
   Like Mamie's on Till's final days,
      Helpless in halting hatred's vibes.

4. I had a fair, dear one before,
      Who sacrificed the only bread
   For me, yet now on heaven's shore,
      Prays my full protection from dread.

5. To honor and acclaim, this sphere
      Set apart a day in its plan;
   'Tis pittance clad, and insult borne
      For those, whose nature nurtures man.

6. Pray I that soon the world declares,
      The love unqualified it gains,
   From those whose endless treasury shares
      With man, the gracious gilts it rains.

51. Mount Of Blessings

1. Each night, just before my bedtime,
    I stop to do a count,
Not of the dangers in my time,
    But of the blessed mount.

2. Quite high and broad in its places,
    Favors I find each day;
Full of joy for love and graces,
    Bestowed, not by my sway.

3. Pals and loved ones are piled up high,
    Atop its stressless days.
Fun and sweet laughter drawing nigh,
    My humble spirit raise.

4. Good health and hours of liberty,
    Add to its beauty too;
That I can hear, think, speak, drink tea,
    Which keep my hopes in view.

5. This mount stands tall for man each day,
    To reckon up his gifts,
In lieu of weighing pains that may
    Highlight his narrow rifts.

52. My Regret

1. It's shameful how I tossed that rag,
        When I did not need her.
    Ragged and soiled like an old hag,
        She'd lost her dainty fur.

2. I thought she could never be washed,
        Once broken and abused,
    By these hands which her dreams had crushed
        And desperate pleas refused.

3. She was picked up by one who saw
        Her intrinsic value,
    And when pure love on her did pour,
        She beamed bright like sky blue.

4. Regretfully, I failed to see
        The heart neath her cotton.
    On each new day, my mind tells me,
        She'll ne'er be forgotten.

5. I was quite wrong for focusing
        On her simple façade.
    Onward, I'll be more discerning;
        My recklessness aside.

53. Naked Heart

1. The sun was hot, the clouds were sparse,
       The day was as if sleeping;
   The scene was slow, as in reverse,
       Seemed all were just awaking.

2. Then came the blasts, from up above,
       This was no celebration,
   Nor was it sign like from a dove;
       Of love, conciliation.

3. It was the start of menace dark,
       And painful for a nation;
   The carnage raw, the horror stark,
       Amid the wild commotion.

4. The dead were stacked in piles quite high,
       Most with their bodies battered.
   The masses ran, through barrage nigh;
       Ensured their hopes were shattered.

5. This is the error of mankind,
       Ever since man was naked.
   Naked aggression rules his mind,
       Because his heart is naked.

54. Nature's Serene Lessons

1. I strolled her lush garden in awe,
        Where she sits on her throne,
    Attended by bright butterflies,
        Yet, they were not alone.

2. While bustling bees the blossoms tend,
        Blithe birds their sweet songs sing,
    And flowers spread their arms in cheers
        For warmth, the sun's rays bring.

3. Proud ants in legions do their part,
        With no complaint or rift;
    Stunning how these dwarfed giants band
        To give their load a lift.

4. Her residents with tenacious
        Energies to deploy;
    Will aid, relieve, and empathize,
        Not tear down or destroy.

5. Shrubs, green grass, trees in one accord
        Share the sunshine and rain,
    While birds and insects raise their young,
        Under her tranquil reign.

6. Her glorious calm can be applied
        In places where men stay,
    Like those which daft disputes and wars,
        Once sentenced to decay.

55. Out Of Darkness Into Endless Light

1. Yesterday's gone, my light has come;
        Into my spring, dark winter's done,
    Summer looks bright, me to become
        The bloom it lacked, its early dawn.

2. Foolish was I, about time's worth,
        Time giving me, much food for thought;
    The wasted loves, the dearth of mirth,
        The hurts my daily dealings brought.

3. I played love's game with arrogance;
        My weakness bared, my armor pierced,
    A chance signal for loves to pounce,
        Surely they did, shredding my head.

4. The friends I made, drifted away,
        Perhaps were not good friends at all;
    Lacking the love that paves the way,
        For triumph's dance at future's ball.

5. Hurtful and sad, my kindred's deeds;
        With darker schemes than darkness spread.
    They scoffed at me, yet pled for needs,
        Their hearts were vain, and spirits dead.

6. The strife is done, all is forgiv'n,
        No time to dwell on erstwhile guilt.
    But center on virtues of heav'n,
        Those the Father, in me has built.

7. Triumphant love has reached my way,
     In blissful peace that would not cease,
   Because my God now has His say,
     In all my plans, and their release.

8. His light on me is bright and bold,
     I rest upon His righteous hand.
   My summer's hot, my seed has bloomed,
     And erstwhile trysts with sin has waned.

56. Path Of Palms And Passion

In His trip, two thousand years past,
     On sun-filled Jerusalem day,
Was met by many thousands massed
     On streets, tight alleys, and byway.

1. He rode that path on humble beast;
     Curious locals and the outcast,
   With thousands to the pilgrims' feast
     Waving palm branches as He passed.

2. "Hosanna! Hosanna!" they cried,
     Blessing, glory, honor proclaimed.
   Thousands too, their fine garments spread
     On the rough, rocky road He strode.

3. On His way, there was much stirring
     In heav'n, while angels kept their watch,
   And saints in their thousands viewing
     Satan's demise, and victory notched.

4. With a tense judge, quite face to face,
   Was charged with treason by His race;
       Thousands, in scornful anger, cry,
       Aloud, "crucify! crucify!"

5. The judge in his weakness complied,
   At soldiers' hands, the Lord was mocked;
       Thousands taunted and smeared His cross,
       Yet He prayed mercy's light on us.

6. He hung; the land saw darkness spread,
   Thousands saw that the sun was dead.
       Others in anguish ran away,
       Confused, and lost for words to say.

7. Lord of the thousands, died alone
   For sins of thousands to atone.
       Thousands must care for thousands lost
       To make thousands trust and be blest.

57. Penned A Book Of Graciousness

1. Penned them a book of graciousness;
       Words woven in love's silk,
   In retort, showed their viciousness,
       Hate hid in iron quill.

2. How can he weave voiceless, and meek,
       Yet, influential words;
   Their hearts inflamed with envy's streak,
       Their tongues brandished like swords.

3. They slashed and gashed, unsatisfied,
        Lay bleeding, my repute.
    Yet, stayed I true and undeterred,
        Gave love—crop of good fruit.

4. Perhaps in time the eloquence,
        Of my words will suffice,
    And soon their angry hearts will sense,
        Love transcends good or vice.

58. Queen That Got Away

Beauteous queen with sensuous lips,
Gracious smiles, curvaceous hips,
Once shunned my moves in her haste,
Missing out on quite a taste
Of a dear love to embrace,
Or for me to make a case,
On her fondness, sweet and rare,
And kindness, special and fair.
Was it something I had said,
Or my charms too bland and odd?
Ponder oft what could have been,
The places we could have seen;
Dubai, Hawaii, and the sea,
Everywhere, just her and me.

59. Quest For The Truth

1. 'Tis odd how those that read the truth,
     Lie to themselves and us;
   For when confronted with the facts,
     They oft stumble and fuss.

2. Often they say, "Tell me the truth,"
     E'en though, in fact they fear
   Wrong emotions could be evoked,
     Through their unwilling ear.

3. Perhaps its cause they know the truth
     As spelled out in His book,
   Yet, ignore its sincere appeal
     In their selfish outlook.

4. Perhaps they are stuck in bondage,
     With eyes blind to agree,
   That holding what is right and true,
     Alone will set them free.

5. Perhaps their inner spirits cry,
     When for its guilts exposed.
   That "those who know the truth are saved,"
     Cannot be presupposed.

60. Realm Of Possibility

All great things I can do, I must,
However small, like grain of frost,
Or quite large like a mammoth's tusk;
Achievable.
All those I cannot do, must be
Like a swig of the entire sea,
Far removed from reality;
Improbable.
Do, I must, great things of reality.

61. Reflections From The Pews

1. That those frequently in the pews,
      Who watch their preacher's show and tell,
   Will e'er abide by the "good news,"
      Is a notion that cannot sell.

2. While absurd expectations soar
      Of those that's privileged to hear,
   The blessings of His love and care,
      They are yet creatures, prone to veer.

3. It's no surprise they're oft in pews,
      Perhaps in light of many flaws,
   Like the oft pious Sadducees,
      Who sadly failed to keep His laws.

4. Amend your blind presumptuous views,
      Of those with chances to discern,
   The good from evil, from their pews,
      For they too have the same concern.

62. Reflections On A Fractured World

1. Think about the world's unity,
   Which seems to be in disarray.
   More nations battling poverty,
   And always in a fray.

2. Think about the bombs men create,
   Dismantling their cities to dust.
   The earthly gods we appreciate,
   Aren't they all a big bust?

3. How about the guns that we make,
   Killing our people, young and old,
   And on the silly drugs we take,
   That quickly make us cold.

4. Then there is the most holy land,
   Where real peace is a fantasy;
   Brothers fail to join hand in hand,
   In love and harmony.

5. What about the class disparity,
   That divides the rich and the poor?
   And for racial equality,
   There is still room for more.

63. Resilience Of The Heart

1. A brother man once let me down,
   A sister pillaged and fled town;
   But these are comrades of my own,
   Whose souls, less maquillage, have shown.
   Yet I am told to love again.

2. Some relatives holding a grudge;
   Their trifling wants, I would not budge
   And others too, their envy surge,
   My perceived progress is the scourge.
   Yet, I'm constrained to love again.

3. Sad, lonely days had been my fare,
   For false and fleeting love affair.
   Loathing or seething, I wouldn't dare,
   E'en when she dots my paths with snare.
   Prone I'm not to indulge again.

4. A spotless lamb shared love with man,
   Through sorrows borne, it was his plan;
   Reviled and crossed by his own clan,
   Though he was guileless through his span.
   Yet, shared more love with man again.

5. Uncertain what the future holds;
   Whate'er may be, what bond unrolls,
   But this I'm sure, this life enfolds
   Distress, and setbacks it unfolds,
   That'll test one's will to love again.

64. Rungs Of Regret

1. I stepped on them on my way up
       Until I reached the top;
    Their spirits tarnished by my boots,
       Their pain from scars won't stop.

2. On my way down, the upset rungs
       Resolved, my mind to tame;
    I fell quite hard to barren earth,
       Much broken and in shame.

3. My fast descent was no surprise,
       For I had lit the bridge,
    To those rungs on my skyward path,
       Who oft my dreams indulge.

4. Cared not a moment how they fared,
       My eyes on what was prized;
    Bothered me not the rungs were wronged,
       Or for what they had longed.

5. Ladders of life are set for all,
       To reach a life's apex.
    Folks must be mindful of the fall,
       When allied rungs they vex.

65. Satan's Loss

A sinner sat on Gabriel's lap,
    The imp said, "he is mine."
The Son appeared in bloodied garb
    With crown of white ermine.

The mad imp melted into hell,
    The sinner praised His name,
And heaven tolled its vict'ry bell
    With saints praising the same.

66. Shadows of Privilege

1. Patronizing open diners,
        My being was spectacle;
    Suspicious eyes tracked each my steps
        To my veiled cubicle.

2. Not that I any crimes commit,
        But my fine crust is dark.
    This movie was oft in repeat
        Where'er his kind would park.

3. Oft, I could hear him whine, complain
        About his fading sway,
    Perceived by his fogged restless brain,
        Though graced with pow'r to stay.

4. No moment would he stop to care
        On my uncertainties,
    Yet, expects I, like Atlas, bear
        His superfluous worries.

5. For long, I'd longed privileges,
        He often presupposed;
    For a taste of advantages,
        He enjoys unopposed.

6. I cannot fathom how he could
        Think soon I'll take his place,
    In a construct that never would,
        His sovereign pow'r erase.

7. In jobs and housing, banking too,
        Chieftains on me, they frown.
    Yet he, they often try to woo,
        E'en with his worth unknown.

8. He must not fear; his privilege
        Is certain, here to stay.
    They will his pallid crust indulge,
        His boon won't go away.

67. Sleep, The Best Sedative

1. Like water to a thirsty stream,
        Manna to mouths extreme,
    Like more scenes to a pleasant dream,
        Your presence reigns supreme.

2. The weary eyes appreciate
        Your respite from the blink,
    And tired brains rush to create
        Visions of things they think.

3.   While broken bodies sprawl across
        Some poor or gilded berths,
     Your perfect peace triumphs the cross,
        They bear oft in their paths.

4.   Deprived of you, the cranky bells
        Ring out in anxious tones;
     Like Lutine snarled in chains which spells,
        Poor moods in mortal zones.

5.   So deep is your sure sedative,
        And deeper yet the jaunt,
     Of those, with rests not tentative,
        Who make up heaven's count.

68. Tales From A Restless Heart

1.   I've never felt true love's embrace,
     Not for love's scarce or barren track,
     Nor its burdens, rife with disgrace,
     But its complex weaves, front and back,
     That daunt this lone and weary heart.

2.   They'll say, "Leave," with a swift goodbye,
     Yet blame me when they choose to part;
     The things unsaid, the silent cry,
     Their secrets cloaked in the night's art,
     They cast upon this puzzled heart.

3.   When love sought its courageous quest,
     My earnest pleas were but denied,
     By those I held above the rest,
     Despite the soul I bared, wide-eyed,
     Denting the love within my heart.

4. Those who cared, whose love was sincere,
   I overlooked, could not foresee,
   If our hearts could ever cohere,
   Merging our souls in harmony;
   Regret now flows within my heart.

5. I can't fault those who did not love,
   Despite my efforts to impart,
   And those I spurned, placed none above,
   God bless them; I played the wrong part,
   Fooling myself about my heart.

6. Love's skill and weave, its tender art,
   In the fabric of every heart,
   I'll learn as life's chapters impart,
   Till doubts on true love soon depart,
   Freeing the chains from this man's heart.

69. The Compass Of Virtue

1. When a heart is where it should,
       With a humble attitude,
   No inducements ever could
       Make it disdainful and rude.

2. Those around it may dismay,
       Fall by wayside in disgust,
   For they dwell in disarray,
       While it thrives by love and trust.

3. Graceful, hopeful, on it goes,
       Quietly in measured steps,
    For it never allows foes,
       Cause its sudden, bad missteps.

4. Patiently, sharing its love,
       With a partner of its kind,
    Heart to heart they daily prove,
       That in one heartbeat are bound.

5. When a heart is where it should,
       Those around it may begin
    To mimic as much they could,
       Its strong desire ne'er to sin.

70. The Crown, A Clever Ruse

1. Perhaps one must concede, the Man
    Did set apart, preferred a clan;
       Endowed with pow'r and upper hand,
       To conquer and enslave the land.

2. Yet His high esteem counters such
    Dang'rous disregard of a bunch;
       His scripted edicts guarantee,
       He does not show partiality.

3. Perhaps wily people agreed,
    A noble ruse and selfish greed
       Would propel to great heights a clan,
       And fit its ugly head a crown.

4. A crown with Kohinoor and more;
   The attributes to high grandeur.
       Purloined from helpless lieges, poor,
       Oppressed by chores and mindless gore.

5. Did divine Man indeed intend
   A clan with riches overwhelmed,
       While subjects its burdens deluged,
       In outposts, its terror there loomed?

6. More trifling is this clan's wild claim,
   Of sole kinship to divine frame;
       Perhaps a smart ruse or abuse,
       Of minds it sets its eyes to use.

7. By wars, the clan builds empires broad,
   Wielding its presumed righteous sword,
       At those natives it deems as foes,
       To infuse fear and lasting woes.

8. Suit yourself, believe what you may,
   In spite of what men do and say.
       No righteous God would dare offer,
       Such pow'r to one o'er another.

71. The Humble Heart

1. I hope that fair people would say,
       Of me: was e'er fair and ne'er proud.
   Whenever he would with us stay,
       Had a way with words, yet ne'er loud.

2. Ne'er lack for earthly wealth like gold,
     Yet ne'er his plenty, fine gold flaunt.
   Oft bringing fair folks in his fold,
     Yet ne'er their feeble feelings taunt.

3. E'er accept folks as they may be,
     In spite of faults that meet his view,
   Urging his soul: bear their frailty,
     Lest these words, "I'm better than you."

4. With kindness spread like morning dew,
     He walked in steps both firm and true,
   In every heart, his love he'd sew,
     A friend to all, not just a few.

72. The Majesty Of The Messiah

1. Thou art the Christ, Son of God the father,
     Sitting on highest heaven's gilded throne.
   Angels and saints profound obeisance offer;
     Pledging full allegiance to You, their own.

2. Thou art the Christ who served many thousands,
     Through wonders of love, Godly pow'r expressed;
   The dead to rise, healing at Your commands,
     That mankind may see, believe, and be blessed.

3. Thou art the Christ who trials oft endured,
     Thriving through fervent pleas and faith in God;
   Yielding ne'er to sin, cravings, and rebuffed,
     Satan's allure of kingdoms in this world.

4. Thou art the Christ, humble and obedient,
    E'en to the point of death on wretched cross.
Form of God, yet conduct not expedient,
    Your name exalted, every tongue confess.

5. Thou art the Christ, who seized hideous Hades,
    That death deters no more man's path to God.
Your promises will withstand the ages,
    By Your sure resurrection from the dead.

6. Thou art the Christ, redeemer of mankind,
    Off 'ring salvation to the worst of man;
Sinners soiling earth with minds quite unkind,
    A path to heav'n in spite of Satan's plan.

7. Thou art the Christ, whose love an example,
    For those who seek contentment, joy, and peace;
Whose souls, Satan's stampede will ne'er trample,
    When from their sin and wicked ways shall cease.

73. The Price Of Principle

1. Soon they would ridicule the thought
    Of compromise and care,
Citing world's hist'ry which portrays
    The gain of wielding pow'r.

2. Cited Peter, Andrew, and Paul,
    Who suffered for their faith,
Claiming their deaths stemmed from blind trust
    In what the good book saith.

3. But what is life if man should cede
        The moral ground to greed?
    Such benefit, life does not need,
        To be at peace indeed.

4. Yes, love, and compromise, and peace
        Exceed the gain of pow'r,
    Wrested by wretched tyrants' thirst
        For more lives to devour.

5. Those who would use hostility
        To achieve venal ends,
    Are often bothered by accord;
        The harmony it tends.

6. Many were harmed for spreading love,
        Like the begotten Son.
    For compromise, I'd rather die,
        The disadvantaged one.

74. The Silent Father

1. As a boy, I yearned for papa,
    Each day, cause I had a mama.
    Found out he had wrecked,
    Mama's heart and stepped
    Out in his wilderness.

2. Late one night, I dreamed of papa,
    Held his hand to get a pizza,
    But when I woke up,
    Fantasies did stop,
    In my sheer wretchedness.

When I needed him most,
So to pals I could boast,
And cover my shame,
Papa never came.

3. She tried to bring me a papa;
   Each one with lustful eyes on her.
   Cried for poor mama,
   Then cursed my papa,
   In hopeless helplessness.

4. Then the coward wrote a letter
   To my uncle at his shelter.
   Said he sorely missed,
   The son he had ditched,
   In his gross foolishness.

   When I needed him most
   To take me by the coast,
   Play with me a game,
   Papa never came.

5. Learned to live without my papa,
   His absence, no more a matter,
   Cause, I ditched the yearn
   And became a man,
   He died in his wilderness.

6. Some kids live without a papa,
   Even though they have a mama.
   Saddens me that they,
   Have to often say,
   "I'm sad and fatherless."

75. The Unheard Melody

1. The bands strummed their sweet songs of joy,
   While people strode the streets in pride,
   Wond'ring out loud, "Who is this boy?"
   Perhaps, their contempt set aside;
   He never asked that he be born.

2. Ragged and worn through much neglect,
   His walk is surely not with joy;
   Seeing them each request reject
   From this stuttering, starving boy,
   Who never said, "Got to be born".

3. This odd nomad at first was wrecked,
   Through carnal tryst, by happenstance,
   Perhaps, some self-seeking affect,
   And he, the living consequence;
   There were no plans to have him born.

4. Did his folks when he first came out,
   Shout, "Gloria! Alleluia!"
   Pleased that their carnal seed did sprout,
   Or with their music, scrammed afar;
   Forsook him then once he was born?

5. Then the bands boldly played their songs,
   He, no more in their clouded view,
   Erased from their erratic minds,
   Whose sordid thoughts this fact did skew;
   It was not his choice to be born.

6. So at his end, the bands played on,
   This time, dirges and marches dull.
   They bowed their heads in shameful mourn,
   With no parents to bear his pall;
   It was a sad and lonely morn.

7. Hope his music plays in each heart,
   Convicting each for connivance,
   Like each failure to do their part
   And safeguard a poor boy's advance;
   Fruitful and blissful when he's born.

76. The Unseen Man

1. Oft expressing how much they cared,
   Their deeds, though, betraying their speech;
   When greed and bold deceit they bared,
   His love and charity did breach.
   They saw his cash, but not the man.

2. In adventures around the world,
   He would oft fund their debt and fun.
   Yet, with pretenses false and bold,
   Played his true kindness like a pawn.
   They loved his cash, but not the man.

3. His honest show of love—like duds,
   In hearts of those he oft pursued;
   His jingling pockets grabbed their heads,
   Yet his soft pleas of love, ignored.
   They heard his cash, but not his words.

4. In his sun, they're apricating,
   Sadly, caring not for his needs;
   Seeing his life true and blooming,
   They sought sole control of his seeds.
   Grabbing his cash—they duped the man.

5. How then is he supposed to trust
   The fateful loves that drag him down?
   Beauty disguised with deadly dust,
   Masking faces with mean eyes, when
   They only see cash, not the man.

77. Their Elusive Mirage Of Affection

1. I've searched their hearts, and watched their ways,
   Rejoiced with them in bright heydays,
   Like in their sun's best shining rays,
   Though they disparaged me.

2. I walked their paths, wearing their shoes,
   They asked of me, sharing my means,
   Yet in my moments of great news,
   Their ghosts are all I see.

   I've studied them, both in and out;
   Their thoughts within, and acts without,
   Each time, my eyes no love could spot,
   Their mirage, all I see.

3. When in my need, their contours change;
   Contriving moves, they well arrange,
   With faces hidden from my range,
   Their shadows, all I see.

4. Said, "I love you," they ne'er replied,
    For much contempt and envy had,
    Those joys with others, perhaps shared,
    Are kept away from me.

    I've studied them, both in and out;
    Their joys within, and moves without,
    Each time my eyes no love could spot,
    Their mirage, all I see.

5. Yet it's alright, no need to pout;
    No need for pressing, or for doubt,
    They know not what love's all about;
    Dark mirrors, all they see.

6. Their cunning deeds are all in vain,
    With fiendish hearts, in so much pain,
    Their envy's loss is quite my gain;
    Ill-will will fail again.

    I've studied them, both in and out;
    Their thoughts within, and acts without,
    Each time no love my eyes could spot,
    Their mirage, all I see.

78. Threads Of Harmony

1. They say, "peace, peace," yet there's no peace,
        We cannot get along;
    Man's warring machines would not cease,
        In carnage all day long.

2. True peace is hard, can't be achieved,
     They cry; so why can't we?
   When slow to speak we are, not peeved,
     In time, God's peace we'll see.

3. They say, "love, love," yet there's no love,
     To share with one and all;
   In spite of love from God above,
     In hate, stumble and fall.

4. Loving is hard, folks don't deserve
     Our love, why try at all?
   He loved, in spite of man's perverse,
     We too must love, or fall.

5. Love and peace, intertwine their dance,
     A righteous life we seek;
   When hearts embrace, not swords advance,
     We will find what's unique.

79. Thrice Tainted

1. Pilfered my life but never lost,
     Save for the tainted thrice;
   When I, the foolish novice caved,
     In their conspicuous vice.

2. Swains as snow whites, thrice appearing,
     Raiding my dainty store;
   Lover, spouse spurious, and lover,
     Good byes! And cries for more.

80. Two Highways I Passed

Two highways I passed,
One, sad sinners massed;
The imp encompassed.
The other, relaxed
With its sinners saved.
To me, the imp asked,
Are you on road blessed?
"Certainly, I said."
"I'll be on your road,"
The bold devil said.
Took His cross I had,
On my brow, I bared;
The imp disappeared.

81. Under the Watchful Sun

1. Strolling around his green garden,
   Greeted by merry birds.
   Eager to face his day's burden,
   Whate'er is in the cards,
   Under the rising sun.

2. Sweating through burning exertion,
   Wishing to make his bread;
   Aching muscles from exhaustion
   Ensure his kin is fed,
   Under the midday sun.

3. Unveiling his barely clad skin
   On white shores of leisure;
   Exposing his darkness within
   In hot spells of pleasure,
   Under the summer sun.

4. Traipsing fraught and perplexing ways,
   When fate defied his plans;
   Shedding deep ties and braving pains,
   His will, at times succumbs,
   Under the scorching sun.

5. Precious hours with great pals and kin,
   His succession secure;
   Weighing all the love he has shown
   With a spirit demure,
   Under the golden sun.

6. Marching alone to the unknown,
   Tipped hats and nods from friends;
   To whom abiding love has shown,
   Which his egress transcends,
   Under the setting sun.

82. Unheeded Prophets

1. Little kids flocked the marketplace,
       Playing tunes with their mates.
   Proud crowds indifferent, did not dance,
       Nor mourn their anguished cries.

2. A man came, neither ate nor drank,
     Preached judgment was at hand;
   He is a strange and dang'rous prank,
     Who's demon seized, they said.

3. Him who arrived, but ate and drank,
     Oft with derided folk;
   Some fraudsters and those of low rank,
     Was called glutton and drunk.

4. Things have not changed through time's elapse
     In proud men's genesis;
   Wisdom in plain view slips their grasp,
     Yet claps to lips of babes.

83. Unyielding Spirits

1. Some have failed at winning hearts,
     That would complement their needs;
   Some have experienced adverse
     Attitudes in words and deeds.

2. Some were spurned for being as they,
     Though the maker did not err;
   Denied access, had no say,
     And their dreams did not go far.

3. Some denied a place to stay,
     Were perceived as underclass;
   Others too, a place to pray,
     Their devotions were en masse.

4. Some were bullied from their land,
    Lost their homes to tyrant's greed;
Giving in to gruff demand;
    But their spirits did not bleed.

5. Yet, over folks' time and space,
    They have ne'er fully succumbed;
With each failure in each race,
    They returned, often renewed.

6. New beginnings always show
    Resilience of human will.
Like Ali would not let go;
    Took a punch but was there still.

84. Veil Of Redemption

1. The earth once clouded by a veil,
    Distressing minds and earthlings crushed;
With much affliction that assail,
    'Twas sad and hushed.

2. Yet, in His mercy thence proclaimed,
    That He will wipe away each tear,
From every eye and grieving mind
    With ears to hear.

3. Sent His dear Son into the world;
    In love, fulfilled the Father's will.
He prayed and preached and fed and healed,
    And conquered hell.

4. In sudden quake, the veil was rent,
     From utmost heights to depths below,
   That man no more a life be spent
     In ghastly flow.

5. And those whom to the Lord will turn,
     Obedient to His perfect will,
   Free from life's strife and evil spurn,
     He will fulfill.

6. The veil from them be e'er removed
     And by His spirit, glory see;
   Where dwells the spirit of the Lord,
     Is liberty.

85. Veils Of Deceit

   The worst share of man's living
   Is when those he confides in,
   On matters of his thriving,
   Betray the trust he's giving.
   Pretending they are caring,
   On whelming loads he's hauling,
   Yet working on his failing
   By scheming and derailing.

   This conning, though quite haunting,
   Much cutting and gut-wrenching,
   Is surely, not surprising;
   Mortal minds can be cunning.
   Even more disappointing
   Are kinfolk prone to lying,
   Perpetrating the trapping,
   To mask their worthless living.

86. Whispers Of The Divine

1. Sometimes He speaks in louder tones,
     Not mumbled but quite clear,
   To listeners in distant zones,
     It is as though He's near.

2. At times, He speaks in measured hues,
     To touch the soul therein.
   'Tis wise to listen for His clues
     And messages within.

3. His subtle guidance sometimes comes
     In moments quite serene;
   A meditating hearer does
     Know what all His guides mean.

4. Can you quiet yourself enough
     To listen for His voice?
   To pray and submit isn't tough;
     You always have this choice.

87. Whispers On My Polished Halls

1. A thought I've heard from kith and kin;
     A spotless house may scare the heart
   Of curious lovers, who may spurn,
     A tidy, pure, and matchless mate.

2. It is a thought that's quite absurd,
     For my balanced and humble mind.
   Mates in no wise could live with turd,
     Save for the brutish, filthy kind.

3. Yet in these walls, secrets reside,
   Hidden beneath the polished planes,
Where love blooms gently, side by side,
   And imperfections find their lanes.

4. In this pristine, gleaming abode,
   Where dust dares not, nor shadows creep,
I find solace—refuge bestowed,
   Where love whispers and memories seep.

5. Perhaps, kin in their judgment drew,
   Such creepy thought; a fishing bait
To gauge my conduct, gain my view
   On their sinister, pointless plot.

6. Perhaps, a spotless place does scare,
   Their cluttered minds and fiendish hearts,
Whose radius has no place to spare,
   For things sublime, with shipshape parts.

7. I, keeper of this pristine space,
   Know that love thrives beyond mere shine.
Mates with pure hearts will e'er embrace
   This place, where dear hearts intertwine.

88. Wholehearted Halves

1. I am a part of her,
   She is a part of me.
Without her, I'm not truly whole,
   She might do without me.

2. She may not be perfect
    In all my varied needs,
But she shares sweet companionship,
    With her oft lovely deeds.

3. I'm fine with giving more,
    Than she can oft afford,
In our seeming unequal love,
    Where we live in accord.

4. Perhaps it's cause I know,
    Love is not always fair;
Oft, one half must do more than whole
    To make a happy pair.

89. Worry's Masquerade

1. Worry does what life's worries ask,
    Oft in form of a task;
While worry sweats, hurries, and balks,
    Worries often relax.

2. Perhaps its cause old worries know,
    That worry will react,
And scurries to fix worries' woe;
    His actions, per their pact.

3. Is worry worth what worries ask?
    This, man himself, must ask.
Perhaps remove old worries' mask
    To see, she's quite relaxed.

90. You are Not Alone

1. When friends and kin your heart deceive,
      Evil to you is done,
   Despite your troubles, must believe,
      That you are not alone.

2. Though rough and dangerous your path,
      In this oft facile land,
   Where fiends will harass in their wrath,
      You're guided by His hand.

3. When shadows lengthen, doubts increase,
      And storms your spirit sway,
   His ample grace will never cease,
      To light your darkest day.

4. Undying love for you will show,
      In spite of all you've done;
   For in the Lord's bosom, you know,
      You're blessed, and not alone.

LIMERICKS

1. Aunt May's Singing

Aunt May, who sang with great feeling,
Was not, in sooth, so appealing.
Her notes, they would stray,
In a most curious way,
And cats in the alley went reeling.

2. Busy With Her Ex

He'd called her number to tell her,
Of his wish to be her former.
But when he called her,
With plans to drop her,
Was with her ex—what a bummer.

3. Can't Tuck It

There once was a man blessed with wit,
Who told his friend, "Please, tuck a bit."
But his friend refused,
His gut quite protrude,
And quipped, "No tucking, I admit!"

4. Distressed

Leisure, for the wealthy, is best,
For the poor, it's a test, she confessed.
Those caught in between,
In toil unseen,
She mused, "Are they not all distressed?"

5. Forbidden Love

In a small town, there lived a wife,
Whose faithfulness was rather rife.
She'd sneak out at night,
With a sly, secret flight,
To eat the forbidden love pie!

6. Hardly A Mayton

There was a man named Ben Mayton,
Who met a dame named May Peyton.
Peyton dates Mayton,
And soon were mating;
Had a boy, Adley A. Mayton.

7. He Couldn't Keep Track

The worst, they said, with a knack,
His trains just couldn't stay on track.
When the boss inquired,
Of the routes misfired,
He shrugged, "Lost count, couldn't keep track!"

8. How About The Weight?

Mister Newton measured with delight,
The beam's tall height and its length just right.
But the force to displace,
Left him in a daze,
'Til the boy chimed, "Consider its weight!"

9. How Frequently It Hurts

He moans about pain, quite frequently,
Claims it's a shock, most decently.
His groans I discern,
For soon I will learn,
It's his puns that hurt, so Hertz-ently.

10. I'll Ask Her

She said it's cold in Alaska,
Much more so than in Nebraska.
So how cold, they asked,
Of the man, who said,
"I am not sure, but Alaska."

11. Inducted was Henry

Bold steps were taken to bar Henry,
From league where they harness energy.
But Henry, quite keen,
To change the routine,
Was inducted, despite the contrary.

12. I See Men's Conductance

He claimed to know men's wary stance;
"Home feuds show dames' strong resistance."
She countered his view,
"Sweeter, dames, it's true,"
And quipped, "I Siemens' conductance."

13. Made Finnegan To March Again

There once was a man from Michigan,
Whose name was Tommy Finnegan.
He marched till he dropped,
Then met one non-stopped,
And followed right back to Michigan.

14. Maize Field

In a field large, he made a maze,
Where amazed kids find their ways.
When lost and dazed,
Quite secluded, gazed;
They're amid maize in a haze.

15. Men; A Fee

There was a man from Menifee,
Who let dames in his park for free.
Men paid, asked "Why so?"
As the dames passed the row.
Said he, "That's the charm of Men-a-fee."

16. Misses Hippy

They called his son, little hippie,
And him they dubbed, mister hippie.
He looked quite scraggly,
His wife, rather folksy;
The crowd then cheered, "Mississippi!"

17. Nadine, The Sleepwalker

There once was a sleepwalker, Nadine,
Who roamed in the night, quite unseen.
She'd cook and she'd bake,
All asleep, not awake,
And wake up—her kitchen all clean.

18. Plans To Meet Her

I had made grand plans to meet her
But lacked coins for parking meter.
When I parked by the bar,
In a no-standing car,
Got towed, thus wrecking plans with her.

19. Priceless Heart

She said I should try to reach her,
But only if I am richer;
Though my pockets were light,
Her laughter took flight,
And love proved the ultimate teacher.

20. Said She Is Blessed Abundantly

She says she's blessed abundantly,
And holds this belief adamantly.
Even when pressed,
She feels truly blessed;
So adamantly, abundantly.

21. Satan Did Not Give Adam

She took the apple to give to Adam,
After the serpent had schemed a scam.
Then found herself bare,
For the scam she did share,
But the serpent, it did not give a damn.

22. Seeta And Geeta

There were twins named Seeta and Geeta,
One in band, the other strummed guitar.
Seeta said to Geeta,
"Please put down that guitar,"
But poor Geeta just did not get her.

23. Stealing From The Plate

There was a church treasurer sly,
Gleaming at church funds stacked up high.
He swiped coins from plate,
Thought it was his fate,
But congregants caught him, oh my!

24. Sumac's Flatulence

There once was a fellow named Sumac,
Whose flatulence was quite a drawback.
He'd enter a room,
And let out a boom,
And every nose would hit the racetrack.

25. The Chemist

In a lab where the chemicals mix,
A chemist was up to his tricks.
With a potassium boom,
And a sulfur perfume,
He found laughter in atoms and flicks.

26. The Cop

There once was a cop from Charm city,
Whose uniform was oft quite spiffy.
He chased after crooks,
In his shiny black boots,
But tripped on his doughnut, what a pity!

27. The Dove

In the meadow, a dove takes its flight,
Feathers soft as the dawn's first light.
With cooing so sweet,
It brings peace to our street,
A symbol of love, pure and bright.

28. The Raving Boss

There once was a boss named Trent,
Whose meetings could never be bent.
He'd talk and he'd rave,
No caffeine could save,
The hours that we all felt were spent.

29. The First Aide

He's always the first aide on scene,
To give hurt folks their first aid, so keen.
Little did they know,
The records did show,
He's why they first needed that spleen.

30. The Yawning Lion

A lion, quite regal and dawning,
Was known for his mighty big yawning.
With each gaping wide,
The mice would all hide,
And the jungle awoke every morning!

31. Their Homes Had Ohms

They judged well when building their homes,
Made them strong within their own zones.
When winds did persist,
Their homes did resist;
They joked, "Our homes have their ohms."

32. They Were from Alabama

"Civil war caused by Obama.
Pandemic caused by Obama."
Said, men in a gang,
With their Southern twang;
All from good-old, Alabama.

33. They Were Quite Diseased

When he erred, oft he was disgraced;
Their acts made him quite displeased.
When they lost their poise,
And their sense of ease,
He surmised they were quite dis-eased!

34. To Maria

Dated a girl by the name of Maria,
Then in Cambria, bumped into Julia.
To wed, I aspire,
But whom to desire?
Dad joked, "Son, it's clear, just marry her!"

35. When Will My Mary Soar

She soared to Maryland's shore,
From Dairyland's wide-open door.
He fretted in wait,
Feared their date was fate,
And mused, "When will my Mary soar?"

36. You Have An Antigen

Dr. says, "You have an antigen."
She says, "Yes, my dear auntie, Jen;
Gets under my skin,
Sickens me within."
Dr. quipped, "You know well your antigen."

Printed in the United States
by Baker & Taylor Publisher Services